The Spirit Connection

The Spirit Connection

How the *Other Side* Intervenes in Our Lives

Dr. Hans Holzer

Author of *Life Beyond, Psychic,*
True Paranormal Experiences, and *Are You Psychic?*

4880 Lower Valley Road, Atglen, Pennsylvania 19310

Schiffer Books are available at special discounts for bulk purchases for sales promotions or premiums. Special editions, including personalized covers, corporate imprints, and excerpts can be created in large quantities for special needs. For more information contact the publisher:

Published by Schiffer Publishing Ltd.
4880 Lower Valley Road
Atglen, PA 19310
Phone: (610) 593-1777; Fax: (610) 593-2002
E-mail: Info@schifferbooks.com

For the largest selection of fine reference books on this and related subjects, please visit our web site at **www.schifferbooks.com**
We are always looking for people to write books on new and related subjects. If you have an idea for a book please contact us at the above address.

This book may be purchased from the publisher.
Include $3.95 for shipping.
Please try your bookstore first.
You may write for a free catalog.

In Europe, Schiffer books are distributed by
Bushwood Books
6 Marksbury Ave.
Kew Gardens
Surrey TW9 4JF England
Phone: 44 (0) 20 8392-8585; Fax: 44 (0) 20 8392-9876
E-mail: info@bushwoodbooks.co.uk
Website: www.bushwoodbooks.co.uk
Free postage in the U.K., Europe; air mail at cost.

Other Schiffer Books on Related Subjects
Growing Up Haunted, 978-0-7643-2895-4, $14.95
From Out of the Blue: A Spiritual Adventure, 0-924608-05-6, $12.95

Designed by Mark David Bowyer
Type set in Myriad Pro / Humanist521 BT

ISBN: 978-0-7643-2892-3
Printed in China

Contents

Foreword

I have written this book for the benefit of people who may not realize that life does not end at death. The late Eileen Garett said that the *Other Side* was another side of life, divided into seven states of consciousness, which I describe in the book. A famous philosopher, Spinozza, once wrote, "God is the same as nature." Knowledge is a great deal of importance, prevalent for dismissing fantasy, skepticism and doubts.

—Dr. Hans Holzer

Chapter One:

Introduction

How Prof. Holzer discovered there was another dimension that we all pass into eventually

I am pretty well established as an author with a long track record in carefully researched books dealing with psychic phenomena. Every case history I have presented in many books and television programs is factual — the interpretation is not guess work or wishful thinking, but the result of corroboration in the appropriate and well-established scientific manner.

One of the principal reasons people listen to me is because of my reputation of being a sensible researcher and teller of true stories. Often, they identify with the people in my reports because similar incidents or experiences have occurred in their own lives, and they find great comfort in the psychic world. It gives them a sense of confirmation: no, they could not have imagined the whole thing — and for that they are grateful.

The bond between the readers and viewers of my books and television programs and myself has been very strong for over thirty years, when my first book was published and I appeared for the first time on national television talking about true ghost stories. My audiences respect the authenticity of my work, and in those instances where I have also produced fictional books or films, I have always clearly labeled them as such, drawing on the true background material of the stories from my storehouse of knowledge in the paranormal field.

My audiences know too, that I will not accept fraud or pretense kindly, and even the well-meaning, but deluded, individuals claiming to channel exotic entities existing only in their own minds have found me less than receptive or even particularly polite in my views of them and their "work." This "middle of the road" attitude, as I like to call it, has at times upset some practitioners of the paranormal, for a true believer cannot tolerate being questioned about the origin or authenticity of his sources and contacts.

Why am I telling you all this, dear reader, when you probably already know it? Because the nature of this new book of mine is such that it requires this explanation, lest you fail to see the profound change in my attitude that has occurred during the last few years, though the portents were there from very early on in my life.

Over the years, I have always made my position in respect to parapsychology and psychic research quite clear: anything is possible, but evidence is necessary. The proof of the pudding lies not in the eating, but in the correct ingredients. I have never had any limitations as to what I might consider authentic phenomena, unlike some of my colleagues who would squirm at the notion that working with mediums could be conducive to obtaining valuable evidence. The late German Dr. Hans Bender of Freiburg University, the "Father of Parapsychology," tried to explain any and all occurring spontaneous phenomena—from hauntings to premonitions to poltergeists—on the basis of a mysterious extra sense developed more in some than in others, but still a part of that person's makeup.

The notion that psychics get information from discarnates, or spirit guides, either directly or indirectly, was totally unacceptable, and to this day still is to some of my colleagues. On the other hand, a psychic magically "reading" another person's mind was eagerly accepted without an explanation for how it was possible to glean "unknowable" information. But in fifty years of psychical research I have never found a shred of evidence that a psychic can read another person's conscious mind. Yet, on the contrary, many psychic predications that have come true were about people, names, and situations totally unknown to the psychic reader and the client at the time of the reading. What the reader does "pick up" is something else, and I have come to call it the Destiny Chart within the aura of the client.

People often wonder about my religious orientation, especially nervous fundamentalists who have been led to believe that all psychical research must be the work of the Devil and his multitude of demons, all, happily, existing only in the minds of religious fanatics, and their leaders. I have always kept my views on religion—any religion—separate from my work as a scientifically trained and oriented parapsychologist because it really has little to do with it, unless, of course, one is a religious fanatic, which I am decidedly not.

I have always had a burning desire to find out all that I could about the facts behind religion, the nature of the *Other Side*, and what the system is all about, but my quest was possible only along conventional and careful delineated scientific lines. This was very necessary if I were to be accepted and my findings taken as the truth they were—and are. Any straying off the beaten path into belief or disbelief would certainly lead into the endless, bottomless, quagmire of assumption without proof. And proof to me is what it is all about, if my work were to have any impact on the world.

After forty-five years of research in parapsychology, I have a pretty solid notion as to what the phenomena are, and how and why they occur. Much of what I learn these days is only further confirmation of what I already knew from previous cases.

Then why this book? Because I have come to understand that there is another reality beyond the one I have been so painstakingly researching for all these years. This is a reality, a system, that actually has firm laws and regulations, and one can obtain tangible, practical results under this system.

Religion has always dimly known of this dimension, but never really understood it fully because religion needed to interpose itself between the people and the system to justify its very existence. But it is also in the nature of that spiritual dimension not to force its way into man's consciousness: man must seek it out himself.

My concern therefore in writing this unusual book (unusual for me) is to share with my audience what I have discovered.

I knew from early on in my life that psychic events were possible. I just knew. My Uncle Henry encouraged such interests, much to the dismay of his mother and father, my maternal grandparents, who were very down to earth people indeed.

At the age of four, while in kindergarten, I caused an uproar by "reading" ghost stories to the other children, pretending I had a book in front of me. Actually, it was only my father's expired monthly streetcar pass, and I could not read in the first place, but the children were fascinated and the teacher was being ignored. This resulted in my mother being summoned, and told that I would have to stop frightening the other children with those stories, or I would have to go to another kindergarten. Now people do get tossed out of college, even high school, but kindergarten? I ceased telling the ghost stories, and the children listened to the teacher once again.

I somehow managed to keep out of trouble during public school, but when I reached the higher grades of the gymnasium — a combination of high school and Junior college — my fascination with what was then called "the occult" got the better of me again. And, it so happened that one of my favorite teachers, a professor of literature, also had an interest in these matters and had written a number of successful novels in this genre. Grudgingly at first, he entered into abbreviated conversations with me on the subject, but I got even when it was time to compose the annual year end paper, which allowed one to rise to the next grade. I was sixteen at the time, and my subject was the significance of Schrenck-Notzing's theory about the origin of telekinetic and telepathic phenomena. Dr. Franz Spunda, without cracking a smile, marked the paper with an "A-", and then mumbled something about my jumping to conclusions. But clearly, he had actually understood the paper.

Many years later we met again in Vienna and became real friends. By now I was living in New York and busy writing books and articles for magazines and newspapers.

Around that time, I happened to pick up an old book dealing with parapsychology, the work of a professor at Tübingen University in Germany. I thought that if what he stated were true, I wanted to investigate the phenomena for myself. Though my major at Vienna University had been in history, my minor was in journalism; later, of course, I studied at Columbia University and eventually acquired a doctorate in philosophy (with a specialty in comparative religion and parapsychology) from the London College of Applied Science.

Now I was in my thirties, and the subject became more and more compelling. Just about then, I heard about a group of New Yorkers who had gotten together specifically to investigate psychic phenomena and mediumship. Before long I joined them. There were newspaper people, a psychologist, a doctor, and of course, the subjects — the mediums. We used the headquarters of the Edgar Cayce Foundation (there was no connection between the group and that organization). On my first visit with the group, I sat in the back row of the small auditorium. Up front on the podium was one of the two mediums the group had met and wanted to investigate.

Betty Ritter was obviously a professional "platform" medium, that is, she would obtain messages from discarnates, relatives, or friends of those present, and pass them on...if they would acknowledge the source. I had seen this sort of spiritualist work before, and sometimes there was certainly evidence, and more often, generalities that would fit almost anyone's dead relative.

Suddenly, Ritter, who had never seen me before, pointed her arm in my direction.

"You," she said, "there is an uncle of yours here for you, name of Otto...and he has a wife, Alice, who's a blond...can you place them?"

I certainly could. My uncle Otto had died in a tragic accident in 1932, his widow Alice, who has since passed over, was then a gray-haired lady, but in his time, she had indeed been a blond.

After this incident, my curiosity was piqued even more, and I subsequently worked with both Ritter and the deep trance Medium Ethel Johnson Meyers, whom

I also met there, for many years. What really convinced me of the mediumistic abilities of Ethel Johnson Meyers was a lengthy investigation, spanning several months, of an alleged haunting in a house at 226 Fifth Avenue, New York. The group was by now, principally, led by Bernie Axelrod, of the *New York Daily News*, and myself.

During the many long sessions, in which Ethel Johnson Meyers went into a deep trance to allow the ghost to speak through her, much evidential material came to light that checked out afterwards. But to me, the most thrilling moment came on August 18, 1953, during routine questioning by me about the house. We had established that the year was 1872, as far as this personality knew.

Who was your landlord? I aked.

Gruffly, the entity replied, not a landlord, it was a woman...Elsie something. I was not particularly impressed, and tried to pursue a different line of questioning, but the entity grabbed my arm, and said, in a tone of annoyance, "but I didn't pay her rent, I paid it to a man who worked for her, collected the rent."

In a burst of bravura, I asked, "Okay, so you paid the rent to her man. What was his name?"

Without the slightest hesitation, the answer came straight and clear. "Pat Duffy...he collected the rent."

Well, after we had concluded the investigation, I went to the New York Public Library and requested their copy of *Trow's New York Directory* for the years 1869 to 1873. I was told the books were not available to the public, as they were being microfilmed at the time. I insisted, and when the director understood my purpose and background, I was given special permission to examine the directories in the microfilm room not accessible to the public. There I found that the house in question belonged to a lady named Isabella Clark at the time.

Elsie is a short form for Elizabeth, and Isabella is the Spanish equivalent of Elizabeth. She then lived at 45 Cherry Street. In the directory for the next year, I found an entry listing one Patrick Duffy, laborer, also living at 45 Cherry Street! Only someone living there at the time would know this!

While my work along these lines continued, I suddenly received a call from Eileen Garrett, president of the Parapsychology Foundation, and of course also one of our greatest trance mediums. Eileen said that she had been observing my work for some time, and wanted me to undertake certain investigations for the Foundation. I was to get a modest grant, and I was to report on haunted houses and ghostly phenomena in the Eastern United States. Over a year and a half, I did just that, hoping to return to my other, more mundane writing work. But this was not to be.

"You must write a book now," Eileen informed me, and one could not easily refuse this wonderful lady.

I did write the book, my first, called *Ghost Hunter*. It was an immediate sensation, went to eleven printings, and brought me television exposure as "the ghost hunter," an epithet I still hear now and then, and which makes me cringe.

From this first book came, at the last counting, 119 more books, though only a part of them dealing with psychic phenomena.

One of the major tenets Eileen Garrett taught me was never to tolerate fakes or vague results in respect to professional mediums. She was as hard on herself as she was on the work of other psychics when they did not measure up to her standards and by that I mean rigid, orthodox scientific standards. Even so, her work in this field, and that of a handful of other mediums, has given us sufficient hard evidence that life continues beyond death, and that communication does occur.

Some years later I was approached by the dean of the New York Institute of Technology, a large private university, to teach a course in Parapsychology. Apparently, there was a demand for it, and since my name had by now become pretty well known as an investigator and author in the field, would I accept an "adjunct" professorship and teach for six to eight weeks a year? Adjunct meant I would not have tenure, but that didn't matter since I had no desire to become an academic teacher. I accepted, and for eight years I taught courses in Parapsychology at both the Manhattan and Long Island campuses.

I continued investigating worthwhile cases now brought to me as a result of my books and television appearances, working with mediums I had personally tested and developed, corroborating the evidence thus obtained under the strictest control conditions.

At the same time, I neither wrote nor spoke too kindly of commercial readers who did not perform adequate work. To this day I sing the praise of deserving, gifted psychics and mediums who do good work, meaning evidential work, and I am the nemesis of the commercial fringe element, from past-lives-while-you-wait practitioners to channelers, to the worst of them all, the "900" telephone number rip-offs.

In *The Directory of Psychics*, I actually graded the performance of psychics I had personally tested or known with the format used by today's movie reviewers of four stars down to two stars. In a vastly burgeoning field, this has become a consumer's guide for those who genuinely want the services of a psychic. As in every field of human endeavor, there is good, bad and indifferent.

I have no sympathy for "demonologists" who travel in the company of a defrocked priest and former police officer, hunting for the Devil in every haunting, instead of helping the people through a proper scientific investigation, and, eventually, with the help of a proper medium, bringing a resolution to the matter. Supporting murderers who claim to have heard a voice telling them to kill, by blaming demons, is of course interference with the proper process, though possession is possible, and I have personally investigated and disposed of cases of possession. But these are discarnate humans doing it, not the Devil and his minions.

As the years went by, and more of my books dealing with true psychic experiences were published and I began doing more television, people knew who to turn to when nobody believed their stories of encounters with what to them often was the unknown. I always answered them, offering help where needed.

With all this avalanche of material and reports, certain parallels began to emerge and impress themselves on my conscious mind.

Truly, if so many of these reports are true as reported (and they were), are they likely to be scattered bits of "exceptions" to our laws of physics, time and space, "special deals" because someone needed to be contacted or informed of the passing of a loved one? Gradually, I realized that these cases were all part of an orderly system that went beyond what I had known, studied, and practiced as a parapsychologist for over twenty-five years.

Carefully avoiding any involvement with religiously oriented groups or movements, even with so deserving a movement as Spiritualism, I evaluated the evidence from a new angle. Not, how do these events contravene or contradict our well-known laws of physics, time and space, but how do these events hang together, and what is their own common denominator.

For years I had been rejecting the Spiritualist concept of "summerland" and "spirit return," based on hard facts that were interpreted to form the basis of a belief system, as being unscientific. Even Theosophy, with its belief in reincarnation, was to me only a philosophy created by Madame Helena Blavatsky in the nineteenth century.

I have lectured at many colleges and universities and helped people in distress over psychic experiences they do not understand — but always in a way that is both rational and truly evidential. Then fear of the unknown vanishes quickly.

During all the years that I actively pursued the phenomena that I was asked to investigate, or when people reported unusually gifted psychics to me so I could test them, verify their abilities and perhaps write about them, my standards were always a matter of evidence: unless knowledge was obtained that had been previously unknown to the psychic, and preferably unknown to me as well, but later checked out accurately, I would not recommend such a psychic to anyone. Conversely, if a case of haunting did not have reputable witnesses and supporting evidence, I would look for other reasons why people had called me to the scene. Verification and specific details are the most important element of an enlightened, open-minded but still scientifically valid investigation.

When I see would-be investigators on television, running around purported haunted houses with an array of Geiger counters, heat measuring devices, infrared cameras, and God knows what else, I shudder. None of this stuff is ever used in real life by properly trained academic parapsychologists these days, and the television "stars" undoubtedly all have day jobs.

People who kept sending me alleged "spirit" photographs were disappointed when I could not see anything unusual in them. On the other hand, I have published a book of authentic psychic photographs taken under scientific test conditions, and anybody looking at them can immediately recognize the faces and figures of whatever is on them, without the need to "visualize" anything. That is the difference between an open-minded scientific approach, and an attitude resting on belief.

It was then that I came face-to-face with the existence of a system — a set of laws — that were totally different from physical law, yet coherent in respect to the phenomena reported. I avoided looking to religious tradition or religious historical fact and interpretation as a source of the answer because, if not for the findings of scientific parapsychology, religion would not have a leg to stand on. But the material, while never fitting into our common physical law of time and space, did, nevertheless, fit snugly into another kind of law — one that is beyond the limitations of time and space as we know them.

This "other" system is as much of Divine origin as is our physical law. The knowledge that a parallel system existed to account for the phenomena I had been recording and investigating made it necessary for me to face up to its very real existence.

In a sense, I came to this conclusion a few years ago with a feeling of relief. No longer was it necessary to try to squeeze the observed phenomena into the rather rigid system we call science, physical science that is. Nor was there any need to look toward metaphysics to accommodate the established, known facts. Metaphysics, after all, despite its scientific sounding name, is no more in quest of evidence (as I understand the term) than religion is.

With that (new) conviction, I also began to look back over years of accumulated material on psychic phenomena of every kind, to re-evaluate them in the light of my new attitude. In the process, I also looked back over my own personal experiences through the years, and to my amazement, I discovered the presence of the system in my own life as well.

Without giving up one iota of my tough scientific attitude towards the phenomena, I now added a second front, so to speak: looking at the material, the reports, the experiences also from the point of view of the "other system," the spiritual system — and everything began to make a lot more sense.

Chapter Two:

The Spiritual Nature of Man

> Man consists of two halves: one physical, one spiritual. How do they work together?

I f we accept the physical aspects of human existence, and there cannot possibly be any doubt about that, we will have to explain the non-physical aspects of our lives as well. But even today there are medical people — those dealing in physiology and with the mind — who champion that "everything" about mankind can be explained satisfactorily from the purely physical point of view.

In fact, some parapsychologists have avoided accepting the notion of another dimension—a non-physical world—that is the home of psychic phenomena, and a connecting link for communications purporting to come from such a dimension. To them, everything a psychically gifted person does in the way of presenting phenomena must be explained on the basis that such phenomena originated in man's physical body and organs, all of it falling well within the conventional view of human existence. Any attempt to extend that origination into areas generally dealt with by religion (or metaphysics, religion's lesser 'brother') is considered strictly outside scientific inquiry of any kind.

But the evidence lies elsewhere, and once the phenomena are looked at dispassionately and carefully, yes, even scientifically, it becomes abundantly clear that the physical body per se cannot produce them within the boundaries of conventional medical and scientific knowledge. It has long been known that man is both a physical entity and "something else." As parapsychology made progress, we were able to give hard evidence that the inner body — the enteric seat of human personality — leaves the physical outer shell at "death" and proceeds to a parallel world in which it continues to function fully without the limitations of a heavier, physical body. Obviously then, we are dealing with two separate aspects of life, joined together temporarily while on the physical plane of existence.

If the "universal law" of physics and chemistry is a firm basis for the development of all things physical in the universe, following scientifically valid and immutable rules, then "the spiritual law of the universe" must do the same for the other component of all life — human, animal, plant — according to firm and immutable rules. But the spiritual side of man is also emotional, and therefore the spiritual law must deal with a value system involving the emotions, actions, and other individual elements, and in this respect it is more complex than the law governing the material universe.

There is nothing haphazard about this, of course, even though each human individual will be considered by the law individually, yet by the same overall standards and concepts. Now we can accept the slow development of the physical universe quasi by itself on the basis of what we know about the laws of physics and chemistry. But when it comes to the spiritual law, we are confronted by some fundamental questions. The first one of these is easy to answer. If this spiritual law exists — and it does — and if it evaluates humans individually as to their spiritual development and actions, some sort of staff, some sort of bureaucracy is required to do this work.

The evidence is firm and multifaceted that people who *pass* from this physical life into the next stage of life, the etheric dimension, or, if you like, "the spirit world," are not sitting around twiddling their etheric thumbs for eternity either. As I understand it, from countless investigations I've conducted, everybody works. Unlike our American welfare system, anyone who can contribute to the system is placed in a position of responsibility appropriate for the individual's skill, intelligence, and development — all of which pass untouched from the physical world into the next.

This of course still leaves unanswered the twin questions of; who is the boss? And who put "him" there? For the moment, let us refer here to God the way we often refer to "the government" without naming individuals, but rather as a principal, a power, an authority. As to who put "him" there, and what was there before "his" time, that is pure three-dimensional thinking. In the spirit world, we do not have conventional time and space, but rather an eternal now, a continuum that flows and never stops.

Lest you consider such notions as purely metaphysical, they are not. Albert Einstein has stated that, at the sub-atomic level, time and space are interchangeable. Our concept of time and space is appropriate for our finite world, our finite physical life spans, and our "local" environment. But common sense would indicate that other inhabited planets in other solar systems would go by their own appropriate time-space continuum, not ours. Time and space concepts then depend largely on the physical world they refer to and regulate. That physical world will differ greatly from the next, because different planets in different galaxies have different distances from their life-giving sun, and thus different living conditions. These very real conditions determine the "space factor" for each world. The "time factor," on the other hand, is connected with the relative age of the planet — how long a period had the particular planet been subjected to its natural physical and chemical influences that are the primary forces of the universe and responsible for all development from formation of the planet to the beginning of life on it.

Now it is probably not difficult to accept and even understand the workings of nature that led to man's existence in this particular world, Earth, in respect to his physical, material self. But we know there is another side to man, a different set of laws, the spiritual side. Here is where man goes astray more often than not, because he is confronted with a system that does not go by the same, safe rules as the system regarding the physical, material world he is more comfortable with. To begin with, the facts are much harder to pin down. What exactly is this other, spiritual side of man? Can we measure it, separate it at death from the dying body? How do the two sides of man interrelate to form the whole?

Man has never doubted the existence of that spiritual component from the very beginning of human existence. Even the cave dweller turned to the Shaman to handle that side of him. The spiritual side also became a repository of anything man could not explain on purely material grounds. The paranormal, the seeming miracles, the ability to reach human beings across distances by thought alone — all of these man knew very early on, but he neither could nor wanted to know how they worked and why. Instead he turned all that over to the Shaman, thus creating a power position for one man that, in the wrong hands, could be dangerous indeed.

To make things even more complicated, early man had no explanation for most natural occurrences, from lightning to storms, from rainbows to earthquakes, from bad luck to good fortune, from illness to fear. These happenings thus became a province of the supernatural, a world populated by a variety of deities, none of whom early man ever got to see directly. Now the laws of the physical universe continue, indefinitely, to shape all that is in that universe, affecting of course man's own development of body and mind across this world's time/space continuum.

Caveman becomes civilized man and civilized man discovers history and acts in it. With his physical skills and his developing mind, man discovers more and more about himself and his environment, his potential, and as he does, his desires increase and expansion of one kind or another occurs. But what about the spiritual side of man? The early Shaman has long yielded to the priest, the gods have gotten more defined and given certain human traits so that the common man might better understand them. The priest defines the system of a supposed invisible world populated by a variety of supernatural entities, and religion becomes a fact of life.

Man is happy to hear that now all he has to do is join a group and go by the rules the priest has set forth. The result should certainly be a give and take relationship between himself and the deities. Some things he wants, he will get — if the deities decide favorably, and some things he won't. It is a comfort for man to have deferred his curiosity about his own spirituality and connection to the supernatural world, to have that reliable spokesman, the priest, answer all questions… But it is not very long before temporal rulers of a developing earth discover another side to the emergence of organized religion: whoever controls the particular religion most favored by their people, also controls the people.

Today, the scientific approach to research in parapsychology is pretty well established. Laboratory "recreations" and artificial conditions to get positive results from gifted psychic individuals, long the mainstay of research originated by the late Professor Joseph Banks Rhine at Duke University in the 1930s, have yielded more and more to competent field research and the observation, correlation, and analysis of phenomena when they occur naturally and, usually, unexpectedly. The enormous body of evidence regarding three types of naturally occurring phenomena cannot possibly by explained away by tortured, and mostly unproven, "alternate explanations."

The three types of naturally occurring phenomena are:

1. The observed apparitions of people after their physical deaths;

2. The direct auditory experiences of witnesses in respect to departed people;

3. Communications, either directly, or through competent and reputable intermediaries, mediums or psychics, that can only come from the claimant in the world of spirit.

To the skeptic, there simply must be another explanation for all this, one that fits within the framework of current scientific thinking and limitations. In other words, what the skeptic is looking for is a way out of having to accept the existence of a spiritual continuity after death, one in which our persona seems totally intact and even happy. The arguments put forth by skeptics – without any regard to actual details of individual cases, usually – are that the perception of an apparition of a loved one after death "must be" due to grief, or if there is no personal emotional connection, and it is a total stranger whose spirit has appeared to a witness, the witness "must be" hallucinating and should see a psychiatrist.

We had a fair number of authentic photographs taken under scientific test conditions that showed figures of spirits — people on the *Other Side* of life — proving of course that their etheric bodies, which they now inhabit, are not exactly made of nothing, but of a finer substance, similarly to the relationship between a heavy tire (the physical body) and its inner tube (the etheric body).

But in order to understand the real nature of the spiritual system, you should fully understand the reality of that *other* dimension — and not on "belief," either! Belief or disbelief have nothing to do with the evidence, and the evidence alone, not emotional leanings, should allow you to accept the existence of that *Other* world, so close to this one.

There's no doubt that religion – any religion – has had an enormous influence on mankind from very early times. It supplied to the average man an edifice that gave him comfort and explained things he could not readily understand about the universe and some aspects of his own nature.

But religion is also responsible for the greatest tragedies in the development of mankind... More people have been killed for the sake of religion, of one kind or another, than from any other cause. Second to it, is fanatical nationalism, but far, far behind religion. This holds true for all religions, but Christianity particularly must bear its share of guilt for having allowed so much cruelty and destruction in its name to occur.

Even at the outset, when Christianity had just become the official Roman State religion, hundreds of thousands died because of a dispute between two interpreters of Jesus' teachings. Was he *divinely* inspired, and a man, as Arianus preached, or was he literally God's son, as Athanasius would have it? The Roman State preferred Athanasius' version because it helped them build a stronger power base, bearing in mind that the Pagan religion was far from dead throughout the ancient world. The Egyptian trinity of Isis, Osiris, and Horus suggested a Christian counterpart in God the Father, God the Son (Jesus), and the Virgin Mary. The latter was shortly to be pronounced to be beyond human laws so that the Immaculate Conception of Jesus could be matched by the Virgin Birth. Now the holy trinity was complete, and people responded to it positively for centuries to come.

Over the years, and through countless interpretations and rewrites of holy scriptures, Jesus became more and more assimilated with God the Father, and to this day, among American fundamentalists, the distinction is not even very clear. The Essene prophet Jesus, the gentle reformer, the divinely inspired potential savior, vanished in the process.

"The word of God" is not totally lost in all religions by any means. It is sometimes diluted, sometimes misinterpreted, or sometimes made conditional upon a kind of "loyalty oath" of sticking to the ground rules of that particular faith.

More and more, over the centuries, man seems to have forgotten that according to Scripture, "God created man in his image." Instead, man seems to have created God in his image. This of course is what the ancients did with their often very human pantheon of Gods. It was both comfortable and represented many aspects of the one and only true deity, which even the ancients realized.

So who is in charge? And who put him (her?) in charge? That, of course, is purely the reasoning of the physical world. And from a physical point of view it is difficult to understand that an entirely different set of laws operates the spiritual system.

God simply *is*, no time or space is involved in a dimension that knows neither. We know for a fact now that a spiritual dimension exists, based not on faith or religious conviction, but available evidence. But a spiritual universe, especially one so well organized and administered, surely must have an intelligence in charge of it — just as the physical universe has authorities.

When I refer to God, it is a little like saying "the government," which does not mean any particular person in the government, but its power, its principle. So it is, I feel, with God. God is the creative power that permeates the spiritual universe, and its highest expression.

The spiritual power we call God is universal, eternal, and positive. It never had an adversary or counter player, except what man has created for himself out of fear. Once we grasp this very simple truth, we are one step closer to leading positive, balanced lives.

Then what came first, the chicken or the egg?

The spiritual universe surely created, "manifested," the physical universe. This view is based on the sequence between the physical outer body and the etheric, spiritual, inner body. Surely, the inner body came first and its physical counterpart followed. And, when the physical body is dissolved at death, the inner body continues right on to function in the spiritual dimension.

Chapter Three:
We Need Not Be Miserable

> *The common complaint: why don't people have better lives? Holzer reveals why and how they can change their lives.*

One of the great attractions of all religions is the hope that through it man can find a better life.

Conversely, man frequently blames his failures to have a better life on a vengeful deity, on bad luck, on curses, on everything and anyone except himself. But it is precisely there where the blame must be placed.

How can a just God allow so much tragedy, so much suffering, so much injustice in our world? If God is merciful, and He is, then why does He permit such conditions? Those are complaints frequently heard and the facts are there to support them. When man is faced with the inequities of life, he turns to prayer for help, to the Supreme Being who will fix things as a special favor. Man rarely examines his own conduct as a possible source of his problems.

This is definitely not "the best of all possible worlds," but a world in great need of change and renewal, a renewal to bring it back to its spiritual roots. Obviously, religion hasn't quite done the job. Progress in technology and inventions of a material kind have not changed the moral fiber of humanity one iota. There are things we can do on our own to change our lives, and there are things we cannot change because they are due to what we may have done in a previous lifetime.

The evidence for reincarnation is overwhelming and I will not belabor this issue. Dr. Ian Stevenson of the Medical School at the University of Charlottesville, Virginia, the pioneer in this field, has written extensively about true cases of proven reincarnation. I, too, am the author of *Life Beyond*, which documents in detail many cases where the recovered memory of a past existence cannot possibly be due to anything but genuine rein-carnation. I have excluded the possibility of telepathic communications, of mediumistic communications from another personality, and still came up with significant numbers of case histories, both old and very recent, that cannot be explained in any other manner. Through years of research and experimentation, I have found that many cases where lives were abruptly terminated in one way or another, lent themselves to exploration through hypno-therapy, and yielded tangible evidence. While we may all reincarnate, it is those whose lives ended in some unusual and often early fashion who are most likely to retain some memory of a previous existence.

The spiritual system demands a balance in a person's passage through a number of incarnations: that which was patently a wrong action in one life, must be balanced in the next. This is achieved by affording the person a chance to do better "this time around." Only by looking at our physical existence as the sum total of all our lives, can we understand the reasons for some seeming inequities and sufferings.

But we also have the opportunity to do something about them in this life. Understanding — and accepting — this concept helps to change one's attitude from despair, anger, and resentment, to one of hope: what can I do to improve my situation in this lifetime? We should realize that the spiritual plays neither favorites, nor does it have a sentimental streak. It applies the law to one and all equally and firmly, and it cannot be swayed by emotional outbursts to "make an exception."

The more obvious miseries in our lives are never in question. But there are other unhappy situations we simply take for granted and do nothing to change them.

• Illness and disease are still treated mainly by conventional medical standards, which concentrate on the physical body with little regard for the underlying etheric body where all illness really starts. Conventional medicine wants to make the sufferer feel better, even if it means suppressing the symptoms rather than attacking the cause. Fortunately we now have some more open-minded physicians who take alternative medicine seriously and try to combine the best of both worlds. A good number have even begun to look at the ways in which our emotional and spiritual well-being affect our physical health. This is a good start.

• We also accept, by and large, the "fact" that our job is not really what we want to do, causing us to be less than enthusiastic about our work. A great majority of people do work that they really don't want to do because they need to make a living. Yet, there are ways to change that. No person should be working at something that is against his inner feelings. We are meant to fulfill our physical lives by contributing the kind of work the *Other Side* expects from us, based upon the abilities and gifts given to us in our bodies, both physically and spiritually. Yet countless people with talents or abilities in different areas — where they would bring good results — never get to use them and instead labor at something they are neither equipped to do, nor happy doing.

When I was teaching at the New York Institute of Technology, I devised a way to test one's choice for the best possible career. This is how it works: Start with six columns on a sheet of paper.

• In the first column, place anything and everything you would have dreamt of being or doing, no matter how impossible or far-fetched — but truly your innermost desires.

• In the second column, place every bit of work you have done to this point in your life, whether for one day or five years, whether paid for, or as a volunteer: all professional or work-related activities.

• In the third column, place the comparisons between column one and two, that is, compare which of your actual work experiences relate to your hopes and dreams. Eliminate what is obviously not supported by what you have so far done in terms of actual work or education, but put down those of your real desires that do have a certain relationship with some of the work you have done.

- The fourth column should contain your estimate as to what would be required for you to do or to attain those jobs now listed in column three, if you had to start from scratch.
- The fifth column should list what you have already done toward your goal of obtaining such positions.
- The sixth column will then tell you what still remains to be done to obtain these positions.

Thus you have refined your desires as to work to the point where you go after what is reasonably possible on the basis of past work and education. I know this system works, as many of my students have followed it with good success. When you do approach a potential employer, in any field, put yourself into a mindset from his or her point of view. Don't tell them what you would like to do. They couldn't care less. Instead, tell them how by hiring you the company would benefit from your skills. Sell your assets in respect to this specific company, and even if they are not hiring anyone, if you do it well, they just might.

Health, Work, Relationships: the three horsemen of the world's misery.

Relationships

When it comes to relationships, it is amazing how many people are unhappy in their marriages or other personal relationships, and do nothing about them. Nobody needs to live a life of unhappiness. God is love, love is happiness. Your fulfillment in the romantic sense depends, of course, on your criteria.

Unfortunately, the majority of people, especially young people, mistake physical attraction as the binding element that promises many happy years together. It seldom is, but that is not why nature has designed sexual attraction to get people of the opposite — yes, opposite — sexes together. Just as the scent of flowers is meant to attract the bee, not for the bee's pleasure, but in order to have the bee carry the nectar to feed itself, and the pollen to other plants and thus help complete the fertilization process, so the sexual attraction factor was meant to "get folks together" for the purpose of perpetuation.

It is the perfect come-on, of course, and rightly so. Looks and personality are undeniably the primary points that arouse interest in the opposite sex. But at this point other factors should be examined as well. The sexual attraction factor was not meant to be a license for promiscuous affairs leading nowhere. It is the physical system's contribution, but the spiritual system also has a place right from the start of an encounter.

Once a couple has become interested in each other and continues the contact, the spiritual development of each of the two parties becomes a matter of importance. If a permanent union is desired, and the majority I suppose would want that, the question of spiritual development is vitally important. If there is total disagreement about the nature of life, about the existence of another dimension beyond the physical world, chances are not good for a happy lifetime together.

A similar, if not identical, philosophy is a must between couples. This is far more important than any possible religious divergence. If they are truly attracted to each other and have found a mutually agreeable philosophy, the fact that one belongs to this church, and the other to another, is really unimportant, and certainly a man-made problem.

Other Compatibility Factors

Next in the realm of compatibility comes the question of work, career, and of course educational and cultural background of the two families. With notable exceptions, try as they might, people from different sides of the track rarely make it work. Man and woman need not have related jobs or careers, but careers they can find interesting between them and can talk about. If the careers are also linked, so much the better.

Also, contrary to popular opinion, age is not necessarily a factor, because we age as individuals, and sometimes quite differently, in biological and mental terms. Statistics, alas, are more misleading than informative.

A rarely considered area where a total difference could jeopardize an otherwise promising relationship is the question of humanity types: introverted or extroverted, diurnal or nocturnal. People belonging to opposites in these areas will have serious problems if they become bonded.

Happiness and peace of mind are possible for the majority of us who are reasonably well. I fear that same majority has too often accepted unsatisfactory conditions in work or relationships as being "god-sent" when nothing could be further from the truth. God does not send us misery — we make our own.

Chapter Four:
The Spiritual
Way of Life

> *There is a spiritual way of life, twenty-four hours a day, every day, and standards and behavior by which you live. In return for living like that you get the benefit of help from the Other Side.*

H aving dealt in the previous chapter in depth with the spiritual nature of man, and establishing that man does indeed have a component other than the physical body, we need to examine how the upkeep and treatment of the two components of man differ. And, differ they do.

To begin with, the physical body has until very recently been considered all of man by a great many scientists of modern times, notably medical doctors. Gradually, thanks to Sigmund Freud, and in some cases still grudgingly, the existence of a mind as separate from the visible organs of the body has become an accepted fact.

But the body always has problems, and the medical fraternity must deal with them. The vast majority of doctors will deal more with the symptoms of illness, in order to please the patient, than the underlying causes. The pharmaceutical establishment goes hand-in-hand with this notion that the body is really all there is, except for that elusive mind that you can't photograph. The remedy is of course a pill or a concoction, usually synthetic, and fraught with side effects.

As for the mind? There are the psychiatrists and psychologists and their often unproven views of what makes man behave aberrantly, and the medical doctors, who look upon mind as some sort of natural extension of the central nervous system. There are conventional ways of dealing with illness of the body, and there are, especially now, alternative approaches of a wholistic kind, treating the illness of one part of the body as an illness of the entire body. In this, they have the right idea.

However, if, as religion teaches, we are "created in the image of God," and God is not likely to suffer from illnesses, how come man is so often ill and less than perfect? Could it not be that the *other side* of man, the spiritual component, has not been properly cared for? The spirit in man may well be the reflection of the intended man in the eye of the "divine creator." That same "creator" may well have intended for man to look after his spiritual side in the proper way. But man rarely does…

God may be invisible and not easy to photograph, but his existence as a power is proven by the very real ways in which his system works. The mind is invisible, too, but the fact that its working clearly indicates its existence.

The average person struggles through physical existence more or less intact, but rarely completely happy.

Whatever negative actions man finds himself guilty of are taken to the Sunday church service, where presumably the slate is wiped clean again, for another week of miscellaneous actions, some good, some neutral, and some bad. There is always that Sunday service, and the majority of humanity has found great solace in the fact that they can do what they want all week so long as they keep going to Sunday church or Saturday synagogue or Friday mosque service. It is a very cozy arrangement, and in their minds they believe it really, really works. But it doesn't.

There are those who reject all religion and the existence of God altogether, and they get their biggest surprise right after they *pass out* of the physical body at death. *Over There*, they get some real nifty schooling, so that they understand how the system works on their next journey to the earth plane.

As for those in the majority who follow one of the world religions, they are on a higher level of ignorance, innocently, of course, than the atheist, but they too, have not yet come to understand the nature of spirituality.

Perhaps I should point out here what spirituality is definitely not. It is not a formal religion or cult of any kind. It is not a philosophy capable of being debated and defended to those who reject it. Spirituality is not an alternate path to being religious. Belonging to a group practicing organized religion, or a solitary teaching of a so-called Master, is still not addressing the core issue of the nature of man in respect to his spiritual component.

The physical body man inhabits for a period is subject to illness and deterioration, though a man who understands the total nature of man and the interaction between the physical and spiritual components will be able to control to a large extent the illness and deterioration, because he understands what the combined components can do in unison, that the physical component alone cannot do.

We obtain our physical bodies from our parents or grandparents. The genes involved certainly shape our appearance and, to some extent, habits and character. But our spiritual component comes from "the pool" of folks who have gone out of the physical world and are slated to return in another body according to the spiritual law, and the law of karma and evolvement of the persona. Frequently, the matchup is less than perfect, but that, too, is intentional so that the person returning to earth learns to overcome discrepancies of this kind. Each and every combination is carefully planned "over there" where nothing is chance or coincidence, but a system that works equally for all, even if some who are its beneficiaries do not always like the results.

The spiritual body is then joined to a developing fetus carefully selected by very competent people on the *Other Side*. Prior to the joining of the spiritual body with the fetus, the fetus is not in any sense "a baby," but merely an extension of the mother's body. Thus, abortion in no way "kills" any soul, any more than a soul may be killed in a car accident or through a heart attack or cancer. The soul remains intact both before and after the death of its physical vehicle, the body.

The spiritual body, made up of finer substance, eventually becomes an inner lining of the developing physical body, and at death, separates from it intact and looking like its physical outer shell. Where so much grief has come to mankind is the lack of realization that this is the case.

Rarely does man pay as much attention to the care and development of his spiritual body, his spiritual component, as he does to his physical self. This creates an imbalance in his existence with all the consequences of lack of interaction between two parts. If we are to achieve a harmonious existence as fully developed human beings, then more attention needs to be paid to that elusive spiritual element in man. This is far from easy: it is actually a lifetime job.

The easy way pursued by the vast majority of humanity is to pour most of our energies into the material life, to look after our well-being, our security, our place in the world; the spiritual side, when it is important to an individual, is then shunted to either the prescribed rituals of one's particular church, synagogue, mosque, or to some other non-mainstream philosophy or belief system. But in either case, it is given specific blocks of time, often routinely, the way we apportion working hours and sleeping time. Only within that particular context are we dealing with our spiritual nature. Naturally, a much larger share of our time is spent on the pursuit of the material world, including perhaps some relationship elements, family, friends.

But spirituality is not a part of man alone ... it is a way of life altogether. Spirituality, simply put, is a definite value system that requires man to pursue his life in the material world not only by the value system of that world, but by the often different value system of the spiritual world. It has nothing to do with beliefs or disbeliefs. It has nothing to do with the fact that you observe your particular religion's rules, such as holidays, fasts, being in the church or temple of mosque on prescribed days, and repeating established prayers. Doing all of those things will make you no more a spiritual person than not doing any of it.

A spiritual attitude, however, will require man to evaluate many of his actions not only in terms of what it does for him, but also how it will affect others involved. Many actions, while perfectly legal and even considered moral by the majority of people, may at the same time result in disadvantage or even hurt to others. Nobody asks that man act like a saint in self denial. But the line is drawn where one person's gain clearly results in another person's loss: here we should carefully consider what is right and what is wrong from a spiritual point of view.

Do not do unto others what you do not want them to do unto you.

A spiritual way of life should not be confused with a religious way of life: no dogmas, no rituals, no obligatory prayers, no must-go-to-church-or-I'll-be-damned. Here are the basic tenets of a spiritually oriented way of life:

1. **Conviction of an Afterlife**. You are fully convinced, based upon available hard evidence or perhaps by personal experience, that there is another dimension somewhere around us, into which we all pass when the body dies. Not on faith, not because your religion told you so, not because that's the way your family or your community feel about it. You don't believe in life after physical death: you are totally convinced it is a reality, and you feel very comfortable with it.

2. **Evaluation of Your Personal Morality**. Once you understand that there is an afterlife, you will become aware of your own position in both worlds and the need to properly take care of the two elements: physical (which includes the mind) and the spiritual. Religion sometimes calls the body "the temple of the soul" ... colorful, poetic, but true. You don't build temples with nothing inside.

So the second important change in attitude concerns yourself. Everything you do, or fail to do, all your actions, your feelings, your whole life in this dimension must now also be looked at and evaluated from the point of view of the spiritual dimension. Does it fit? Is there a discrepancy? Is there a conflict? Often there is. Sometimes you may have to choose, and if you choose the right course of action in terms of morality, fairness, justice, compassion — then you will know what to do. For example:

• You are a passionate hunter who loves chasing and killing animals for sport, not because you need their meat to survive. But animals are fellow creatures of the same spiritual world. Your motive is not compelling; it is selfish. You will give up the hunt and find other, innocent outlets for your need of excitement.

• Someone you know asks for your help, not in monetary terms, but counsel, and a little of your time. There is nothing to be gained by you in doing it. You are extremely busy pursuing your own career. Even a brief interruption of your schedule might be difficult to manage. But you overrule the practical monster, and you help your friend. That is the proper spiritual way.

3. **Relinquishing Fears of the Unknown**. When you have accepted the continuance of life beyond physical death, you will find your fears of the unknown are beginning to vanish. By now, hopefully, you have overcome your particular religion's teachings about heaven and hell, and sin, and punishment in the hereafter. All of these are distortions designed to keep the members of the group in line. The *Other Side* is neither heaven nor hell, but a spiritual continuum, where everybody passing into it finds his proper level and place — up or down. Of course, what you do in this life matters, but not because you will appear, after death, before the throne of the Lord and be judged, and punished if you deserve it. What we call God, is All Love, and to the degree we can absorb it, we partake of that love.

4. **Your Spiritual Schedule**: 24-7-365. You no longer divide your week into a work week, when more or less anything goes, and a calmer weekend, where you go to church or synagogue or mosque, and atone for your trespasses, so you can start fresh on Monday committing them again. Your spiritual orientation is active and alive seven days a week, twenty-four hours a day. Yes, twenty-four hours because in your dream state you sometimes exteriorize suppressed conflicts and confront them.

5. **Knowing Your Place in the Universe**. Nothing in the spiritual way demands sacrifice from you, unless your actions will clearly hurt another person or animal. To the contrary, a totally spiritual outlook will enhance your ability to succeed, to enlarge your horizon of knowledge, to bring you greater success, because it frees you from the terrible conflict of the struggle for survival and success against what is often a hostile environment. Being spiritually attuned, you will know that all things proceed as they are meant to under the universal law, and you need only do your part properly and at all times.

6. **You Are in Control**. Man has a higher nature and an animalistic body derived from lower sources through evolution. Spirituality does not mean suppressing that animal nature, but it does mean controlling and balancing it within the concept of a responsible and positive lifestyle. There are no commandments, really, no threats of a dire kind if you fail or slip. Only you in your own

heart know that. You are, in fact, totally in control of your actions and reactions in this life.

7. **God as the Universal Force**. When we refer to God, we really do it the way we speak of "the government": a force with many ways to appear. Thus it is with God, in whatever form He takes for you, that you are really referring to as the supreme power that works with and through many, many beings; some like to call them angels, others spirits, or spiritual guides. But they were all in physical bodies at one time, or several times around, and are not supernatural fantasy beings created by the religiously oriented mind to fit into preconceived imagery, regardless of the hard evidence.

8. **Spirituality is Natural, Not Supernatural**. Nothing in the universe, either the physical or the spiritual, is anything but natural. Not integrating your spiritual half into your being is being less than natural, less than what nature, or the Divine, wants you to be.

Spirituality, then, is a fuller understanding of what you are, what your powers and potentials are, and how to make best use of them: for everyone has a destiny to fulfill on earth. The system supplies the opportunities, but you decide to take them or not. This is called 'Free Will' and is also part of the Divine Master plan, as I see it. You must contribute something of yourself in making such decisions.

9. **Nourishment and Spirituality**. Lastly, but perhaps most importantly, the maintenance of the physical body in a certain manner has a great deal to do with the Spiritual Way of Life and its benefits. At the most

desirable level, man should not partake of any food or drink coming from animal sources, containing synthetic substances or chemicals, and if necessary make up deficiencies in the nourishments, if any, with organic or holistic vitamins and minerals.

This is called the Vegan diet and its benefits have a great deal to do with considerably healthier and longer physical lives and the absence of illnesses, most of which are caused by toxic substances taken into the body. Animal-based products of any kind are the main culprit, apart from the moral issue of taking lives — any lives. For some individuals this may be a difficult decision to make, but the earlier in life it is made, the stronger will be the impact, and the results.

In order to lead what I have come to call a proper spiritual life, we don't follow written rules, strict laws, and orders found outside of ourselves. We need to find them within us, and live by them, even though nobody — not even God — insists we do. To do this properly, and exercise good judgment over all our actions, thoughts, and feelings, we need not go to any school, or read a catechism or any other book assuring us it contains the right formula for us.

When we arrive in any incarnation, we are already equipped with a thirst for knowledge, some people more, some less, but all have it to some extent. What each individual does with it is another matter. Each has free will and can of course totally ignore it and lead their lives accordingly. That, too, is their birthright. But those who want to make a better life for themselves and more closely approach the human being "created in God's image," can do so on their own, without help, even without the need to pray for it.

Any thinking person has at the very least a rudimentary understanding of what is good and what is evil in this world, what it means to help others and what it means to contribute something to the world that will perhaps make it a better place to live in. Those are fundamental truths, and those who violate them know full well what they have done. We ourselves create the spiritual quality of our physical existence.

What about criminals and demented people who cannot or will not accept the need for such concepts? Free will works both ways: the criminal, a result of many factors in both this life and an earlier one, chooses not to fight or overcome his inclinations. The demented person cannot of his own will find the way to *The Light*, to the degree they are capable of.

For just as God is all love, and not the threatening, punishing God of the scriptures, so is man not born with "original sin," as the church would have us believe. Man is born free, with the built-in potential to be good. Any guilt he acquires on his progress through life, he has only himself to blame for.

A "good" man recognizes his place as part of the human race and the responsibilities that come with it; not just to do well for himself, but to be an active contributor to the world's progress, to the extent he is able to. A man who does not pay attention to that responsibility is not necessarily bad, but he does not fully lead a spiritual life.

Only someone who wants to change his life to a spiritually balanced existence may have his prayers answered. If an increasing number of people all over this planet were to realize this, and accept the need for a spiritually balanced life as a basis for future good health, success, and happiness, as the Deity intended it to be, then perhaps some of the great evils rampant in our world today would not exist or continue to exist.

You cannot come to this state of affairs except by the conviction that it is indeed the right path for you. It is a highly personal decision, and it involves a new direction in thinking, action, and feeling. But it would make a difference, all the difference, in the world we live in.

War, that is shooting war, would not be possible. Force would have to be applied to deal with evil, but not to the extent of wantonly killing human beings. Cheating of any kind and type would not be compatible with the spiritual way of life.

Am I talking about a utopian world? Yes, of course, unless mankind turns en masse to spirituality as the "other half" of their existence, and from within, by themselves, would see their world with different eyes... the rest would fall into place, step by step. This is not a new faith that can be preached on television and in big arenas. It comes from each and every individual, and only because they want it, and accept it, of their own free will.

In other words, spirituality is not a religious orientation, a new philosophy, a new anything. It is a way of life, holistic life, if you wish. It is an attitude towards life, towards your fellow human beings, towards your responsibility as a member of a universal community called the human race. It does not recognize geographic boundaries, differences of religion, differences of race or age or even culture. Its main tenet is that we are a spiritual being encased temporarily in a physical body, and that we are to act accordingly, not merely from the physical body's point of view.

Once you have reached this conviction, and even if you have lived differently before, you are on your way to understanding yourself better, and by embracing the spiritual way of life, gain access to all the benefits that come with it. There is no membership fee to join, only sincerity and persistence, and you are not expected to sacrifice anything.

If you like the good life in this, our physical world, fine, so long as you are not hurting others by living it. Selfishness, greed, intolerance, violence, vengefulness, and immorality (in the basic sense) are no longer part of your way of life, or should not be. The spiritual way has no quarrel with physical pleasure or enjoyment, with wealth and success, and even power. But the proviso of not getting benefits at the expense of others' sufferings or losses still holds.

Chapter Five:

The *"Other Side"*

What exactly is that 'Other Side'? And where is it?
Dr. Holzer has the answers.

few years ago, I was walking on a beach near Santa Barbara, California, in the company of the Bishop of California, James Pike. He and I had been friends and at that moment we were discussing his latest book of non-fiction, dealing with the amazing contact between his dead son and himself — a contact that had convinced him that there was indeed another dimension beyond this one, into which we pass at physical death. Since we were at the time both published by Doubleday, he sought out my opinion on what to call this very important work. I knew about the case and had been with the bishop in England making a documentary film about it.

"But what shall I call the book?" Jim asked. He looked at me.

"Call it 'The Other Side'," I replied, and evidently I had hit pay dirt. He loved the title.

"Yes, yes," Jim said, eagerly, "the *Other Side* of this and that, *The Other Side* of my story, what people will think of it."

But then he stopped and looked at me with a very serious expression. "That is where my son now lives. On The Other Side."

And so it happened that the term was born, and the book was named. It was a great success.

From then on, Bishop Pike took a great interest in parapsychology and the evidence for the existence of that 'Other Side' of life.

People without much knowledge of the evidence, which has piled up over the years, about the reality of world beyond this one, will shrug off the question about the nature of that *Other Side* with the old crack, well, nobody has ever come back from there to tell us. But they have, in droves...

There are, first of all, communications between relatives or friends who have passed over and have in one way or another been able to get in touch with someone over here. The vast majority of genuine communications between discarnates (spirits) and people in the physical world is initiated by them, not by us. We can open ourselves up through meditation and prayer to receive, perhaps, a communication with a loved one, but it only happens when that person gets permission to communicate. That permission is given when the "administration" finds the reason for the desired contact both legitimate and in the interest of both parties.

Gifted, genuine trance mediums can make contact possible, especially when a troubled personality on the physical side needs to have contact to understand his or her true situation, and in order to be free and able to cross over to the *Other Side*. I have done this work for years with the help of a few – a very few – deep trance mediums who had the gift.

People troubled over here by the loss of a loved one sometimes consult mediums in the hope of getting some sign of their continued existence as individuals, and a really good medium should be able to make contact, though by no means always or easily. The personality on the *Other Side* — a normal individual, not in any way a "ghost" — will still require the permission from his guide personality to allow the contact.

How do I know all this? In forty-five years of intensive research and investigations, I have of course had many cases where communication was the key issue. In an astonishing number of cases, in widely scattered areas and at different times, reference was made by the communicating personality, that he or she "must go" now, because the "big man" or the "big fellow" was telling them to. Time's up!

The reason? An enormous amount of energy is expended in the process by the trance medium, and when that energy seems to run out, the supervising guide will call a halt to the conversation. Similarly, when unsought apparitions who have managed to make contact with a living loved one have exhausted their supply of energy, even including the usual contribution by the percipient as well, they will take their leave and vanish.

Nothing in any universe works without energy, and the spiritual system also uses energy to operate, an energy not unlike electro-magnetism called the aura, which we all have in our bodies when in the physical state.

The vast majority of these contacts reaching out to us over here from the next dimension are motivated by one of three reasons. It may be simply to reassure the people they left behind that death is not the end, and they are well, or that something on the earth plane has not been done right in respect to their passing. Or it may be to help their loved ones in some difficult circumstances, almost like deputies of the "professional" intervention people doing this sort of thing as part of their assignment on the *Other Side*.

In each case, they make sure they are clearly recognized as to who they are and the witnesses never doubt it. As to their appearances, they usually appear as they were in life, perhaps a little younger and healthier look, but essentially themselves. The dead do not sprout wings or walk about in shrouds, except of course in some Hollywood movies.

Contact from the *Other Side* by the people who have passed into it is never frivolous as their laws would not allow it. There must be a useful purpose in "getting through."

Lest my reader remains unconvinced of the reality of such contacts, here are some typical ones of recent vintage immemorial:

• A security guard by the name of Don McIntosh of Washington State had not the slightest interest in psychic matters, but when he woke up one morning, he had the distinct feeling he was not alone in his room. It was just 6:30 a.m. on this November day, and as he rubbed his eyes, there at the foot of his bed he clearly saw the face of his California cousin.

"Don, I have died!" the cousin said loud and clear, and then the face vanished.

While Don was still discussing the extraordinary event with his wife, wondering whether or not they should contact the cousin in Ventura, California, the mail was delivered. In it was a letter from California, containing the news that the cousin had died a week earlier.

• The second cause for contact is well illustrated by the case of the music teacher Bernard Mollenauer, whose mother Frances had died rather suddenly of a stroke. As per her will, she was cremated, and her ashes placed in a niche at Greenwood Cemetery. But a month later, the mother appeared to her son, complaining bitterly that her ashes had been mislaid. The son refused to believe this could happen and even argued with his late mother about it. But she showed him, in his vision, a little table with a wire basket containing a small copper container.

The next morning, Mollenauer tried to convince himself that he had dreamt the whole thing, but he nevertheless went to the cemetery. There he discovered that his mother had been absolutely right. The ashes had never left the undertaker's place, where they were in a little wire basket on a table, just as she had said.

Cases where the person on the *Other Side* intervenes on behalf of someone over here (undoubtedly with permission from the appropriate authority on the Other Side) also indicate a close continuing interest by them in what happens to us over here.

• The actress Gloria DeHaven was driving on a country road in California during a heavy rainstorm. It was pitch dark and she could scarcely make out the road before her. Suddenly, there appeared on her windshield the face of her late mother, staring at her with an expression of alarm. The sight of her mother so startled Gloria, that she stopped the car immediately. Instantly, the mother's face disappeared from her windshield.

Gloria decided to take the opportunity to check out the condition of the road ahead. As she got out of the car, she realized why her late mother had made the contact with her — just inches ahead of where she had stopped, the road was completely washed out. Had she continued to drive for even another minute, she would have been swept down an embankment and to certain death.

• Many years ago, when I lived in a high rise building on Riverside Drive, I often worried about getting dizzy by having my head in the wrong position when I slept. Real or not, it caused me always to sleep on two pillows. One night I woke, and in the dim light coming in from the window, I saw my mother, dressed in white, pushing my head back onto the pillow from which it had slipped. She vanished instantly when my head was back in the proper position.

Many who pass over, perhaps even the majority of people, either have false notions of what to expect at death due to religious brain washing about heaven and hell, or they expect absolutely nothing what-so-ever — death would be the end.

Such was the case of my brother's father-in-law Leon, a businessman who thought my studies of the paranormal were pure nonsense. Leon died, suddenly, of a heart attack while riding on a bus, and left a very distraught wife behind, a lady who had never really looked out for herself to any extent and had always relied on his counsel.

Several weeks after the funeral, I happened to be in my kitchen at four in the afternoon, preparing coffee. All of a sudden I felt someone close to me, and I clearly heard my name called in an urgent tone of voice. Always the cautious investigator, I ran to the other end of the apartment where my wife was seated reading a book, and asked if she had called me, which she had not. Then it occurred to me that even if she had, her voice could not have been heard on the other end of the large apartment where the kitchen was situated.

I dismissed the matter, but the following day I was again in the same spot at about the same time, when it happened again. Only this time I clearly recognized the voice as that of Leon, who had a peculiar way of pronouncing my first name, quite unlike anybody else. I realized that it meant for me to call his widow. I did, and found her in a state of total depression, thinking about suicide. Immediately I explained what had happened, and though she was not prepared by her upbringing to accept survival beyond physical death, she was willing to listen. My call did make a big difference. Leon has not communicated since, and his widow has long since joined him *Over There*.

We are of course speaking here of people who have had reasonably normal transitions to the *Other Side*. When something goes wrong, and a person dies in shock or under traumatic or other emotionally unacceptable conditions, the transition cannot take place and the individual remains in our world, though no longer properly part of it. The result is often panic leading to what science call poltergeist or physical phenomena, which are nothing more than desperate attempts at communication from a spirit who cannot understand what has happened to him. Popularly called "ghosts," they are simply people who need help to go on to the *Other Side*, where they will also be received and treated properly for their emotional disturbances.

"Ghosts" then, are not able to freely communicate, and those who wish to help free them as a result of reported disturbances in a house or place, will deal with the entity, usually through a deep trance medium, the way a psychiatrist deals with a patient on the physical plane, trying to convince them that they must go on, to call out to their loved ones to help them make the transition, and generally calm their panic and apprehensions. I have done this work many times, usually with rapid success. Amateurs, however, should never attempt it as they can harm the entity immeasurably by not being cognizant of what is possible, and what must not be attempted.

Whatever information I possess about the nature of that *Other Side* is not theory or my own opinion, but a composite picture based on many years of investigations, many different cases, and what the communicators have said in them. This applies not only to the communicators, the discarnates who have passed on to the *Other Side* and are well adjusted to their new life and assignments, but also to their superiors or administrators — people who are placed in charge of monitoring and clearing communications and who sometimes are referred to as guides. The ordinary communicators have often referred to them as "the big fellow" or "the big man." These bits of information have come from widely scattered areas and all sorts of individual communicators for many years. There is no reason to doubt the accuracy of their statements.

What is the *Other Side* like? As solid a world to those who live in it, as the physical world is to us here. The differences are lack of illness, an absence of finite time as we know it, and total control over one's actions, movements and appearances through thought processes only. Withall, these people do not float around in spirit robes, though some undoubtedly have so chosen, but usually are duplicates of their best physical selves, operating through a finer, enteric body that had always been hidden underneath the duplicate, outer physical one.

The *Other Side* is a complete world also — anything human beings are used to in terms of environment exists there, too, and even though the creating force is thought energy, the houses, trees, roads, clothes, books, everything they use or like to use are solid to them. There are of course discarnate animals, pets especially, and plants: it is a complete world.

The difference becomes obvious only when a visit is attempted from there to here. This is a reverse trip through a tunnel and involves lowering the vibratory rate from the high rate of the spiritual world to the slower, lower rate of our denser physical universe. As they approach our end of the tunnel, they can see us as if through a fogged mirror, but of course once they have left the tunnel, and are temporarily in our universe, they see very well as they did when still living in the physical world.

Now about that tunnel…

In recent years, Near-Death Experiences have been reported in increasing numbers. These are situations where someone has an accident or illness, and is suddenly projected out of the body, yet not totally separated from it. The reports are universally the same. The person finds himself traveling at increasing speed through a tunnel filled with bluish-white light, and eventually encounters friends or relatives who have passed on before.

At the end of the tunnel, there is a person halting his further progress. This is either what people often describe as "a being of light," or a known relative. Inevitably, that person will stop the traveler at this point and tell him to go back, "because it is not your time yet." The traveler has no choice, and usually is rapidly sucked back into the tunnel in the direction he came from eventually spinning around as the vibratory rate is slowed down and he can re-enter his physical body.

On awakening, the entire experience is fully remembered. It differs from ordinary out-of-body experiences that usually occurs during sleep or sometimes during anesthesia in hospitals; the latter does not involve any tunnel and is simply that — out of the body experiences during which the percipient can clearly see his limp physical self underneath, as he floats above it, and of course eventually snaps back into it.

Try as they might, conventional medical people cannot explain the near-death cases on the grounds of hallucinations, shock or other "acceptable" causes. Too much serious research, including some of the more open-minded medical doctors, have proven these experiences to be real and exactly what the person who has gone through them says they are.

How is it possible that near-death experiences occur in what appears to be a completely fool-proof system, the spiritual system? While the spiritual system does indeed make mistakes, the physical world is full of them. Accidents happen because of various circumstances, from karmic needs, to human failure. The spiritual system does not control our every action. But it does deal with action resulting from a physical situation, such as an accident, that causes a person to arrive at the next stage of existence when he is not due. So back he goes.

This of course means that we all have a due date and that those on the Other Side, some of them in certain positions, know them. What determines the day of our demise is a highly individual matter, and I can only guess that this is determined by the leadership on the Other Side based upon an individual's track record, usefulness to the world while in the physical state, karmic debts, and other elements that make up a person's "profile." It would indicate a system where every week is planned, determining our life span in the physical world by spiritual values. During that period, the personnel on the Other Side will carefully monitor our progress and intervene when that is indicated.

I don't think this attention to individuals is the same or of the same intensity with everybody any more than everybody being the same. Some people may not even be "on the list" because they cannot go beyond their limitations in this lifespan, while others are of greater interest to the Other Side because of their potentials in terms of spiritual values. After all, we over here, or some of us at least, represent a kind of investment, and they are looking after it.

Near-death experiences can best be accepted when we consider that near fatal accidents, for instance, may be "scheduled" to occur in someone's life, but the outcome is not set in accordance with free will and the margin, even the karmic law, allows for individual decisions and actions.

If everything were totally predestined, we would be mere automatons, and it would be quite necessary for us not to make any efforts whatsoever since the outcome had already been decided upon by a higher authority. But this is simply not so. All encounters, whether with situations or people, are set up long before they "happen" to us — but not the final outcome. Only in very few cases, where the outcome has been necessitated by a karmic debt of some kind, will the action or reaction of the individual concerned be of no avail. Of course we never know which type of situation we are confronted by and this is also as it should be. The spiritual system plays it close to the vest. We must always expend our best efforts.

No two near-death experiences are totally alike, but they all have one common denominator: go back, you are not yet due "over here."

• Ms. Virginia S., a housewife in one of the western states, was having an operation to repair a muscle, but somehow, she lost so much blood that she was actually clinically dead. Nevertheless, the surgeons frantically worked to bring her back, and in the end, they were successful. During that period, Virginia found herself climbing a rock wall, straight in the air. At the top of this wall was a stone railing about two feet high. She grabbed for the edge to pull herself over the wall, when her late father appeared and stopped her. "You cannot come up yet, go back, you have something left to do." Virginia looked down, and the next thing she remembered, was waking up in the hospital.

• The famed Israeli bio-energetic healer Ze'ev Kolman had such an experience when he was a little boy. While visiting his father in a work camp, he ran off to play and accidentally fell in such a way that he hit a stake very hard. He became instantly unconscious and found himself floating in a tunnel, filled by purple-blue light. At the end of the tunnel, there was a bright light. Then there was his grandmother, holding up her arm to stop him from going further. "Go back, child…it is not your time yet." With that, Ze'ev was sucked backwards through the tunnel, spinning as he went along. Next thing, he awakened on the ground, safe and sound.

Not all near-death experiences involve the tunnel, but a large number of them do, and there are some very competent books available discussing these cases. Clearly, we have a certain target date for the transition and the Other Side does not want us to arrive any sooner. We all remember several versions of the play and film "Here Comes Mr. Jordan," or "Heaven Can Wait," about a young man "accidentally" pulled out of a car wreck by his "angel" before he was really ready. The angel then had to find him another body until it was his time. That of course is pure fantasy. But it is fact that you will not be on an airplane that the Other Side knows is doomed, unless you are meant to "go." They will manipulate ways of keeping you off that plane, from "hunches" to psychic predictions by someone you trust, to making you change plans in some manner.

Even when two people travel together, and there is an accident, but only one of you is marked for death, they will intervene.

Mrs. J.L.H. of British Columbia was driving back from her stepfather's funeral. She was riding with a friend, Clarence, when there was a terrible road accident. Clarence was killed instantly, and Mrs. H., who had just caught a glimpse of the lights of an oncoming car, was hurt. She looked up from the wreck, and there was her late stepfather, "stepping forward out of a cloudy mist." He touched her on her left shoulder. "Go back," he said, "it's not time yet." She clearly felt the weight of his hand at her shoulder.

The *Other Side* then, it appears, is a well organized world in which those who pass lead constructive, even busy lives according to their abilities, desires and spiritual development. No two people are alike in that respect, but the spiritual dimension accommodates them all at their respective levels.

In a recent work, *Life Beyond*, I have told of true cases where living people have visited with their loved ones in so-called dreams or visions, and found them quite happy, well and busy. Since such reports came from other sources too, and could be correlated, it would appear that they do represent the state of the reality on the *Other Side* accurately enough.

Now we know a good deal about the *Other Side*, the system, and those who operate it, people who have gone over before us. The question that is far more difficult to answer is the question of origin. We know fairly well how natural chemical reactions have led eventually to the physical world we know.

Did the spirit world also grow "by itself" out of simple beginnings? What about God? Creation? Angels? Devils? Heaven and Hell? Purgatory? Salvation?

Chapter Six:
Conditions
on the *Other Side*

What is life like beyond "death" of the physical body? You'll be surprised at the answer and the details of life after "death."

B efore I can discuss how the *Other Side* intervenes in our lives, we need to know more about that "Other Side of Life." Fortunately, the information, in very concrete terms and not in vague, philosophical, or heaven forbid, quasi-religious terms, is available at this juncture. A good researcher will always look at all the available evidence, coming from as many reliable sources as possible, and then compare the material, searching out similarities, and, of course, differences.

In respect to the nature, system, and way of life on the *Other Side*, my primary source to draw from consists of three elements:

1. The reports of other researchers when describing the conditions prevailing on the Other Side based upon the testimony obtained by them through responsible, professional mediums, and in some instances, amateurs, that is non-professionals, who are nevertheless capable

of mediumship of this kind. The mediumship I am talking about is generally known as trance in which a spirit person will communicate with the medium directly, the medium, however being in a state of trance when his own personality is temporarily set aside.

In a new book I have co-authored with the celebrated medium Philip Solomon of England, some two hundred such interviews are to be found with people in all walks of life, and based upon a specific set of queries drawn up by me to elicit as much detailed and realistic information from these interviews, in trance, as possible. When I compared these "protocols," I found, to no particular surprise, that essentially all of them described the nature of the *Other Side* in identical terms.

2. An important second source are the statements obtained from individuals who had experienced near-death incidents and had returned to the physical world afterwards. Nowadays such experiences are no longer relegated by physicians and other researchers to "hallucinations," but taken at face value, and the incidents have been carefully evaluated in a proper scientific manner.

3. The third element furnishing us with information about the nature of the *Other Side* was Astral Projections. What we used to called Astral Projection is nowadays usually referred to as out-of-body experiences. They differ from near death experiences in that the majority of them are induced rather than accidental, though not all. Certain physical conditions, such as anesthetics as part of planned surgery, or emergencies requiring surgery, have often led to temporary out-of-body experiences, with

the subjects usually recalling clearly what they observed. In many such instances, the patient will get "a glimpse" of the *Other Side*, see "dead" loved ones reassuring them, but will come out of that state as soon as the surgery has ended. At best, such individuals can report fragmentary evidence about the appearance of the *Other Side*.

Taking all this material and running it through my mind's "computer," I have a pretty clear picture about this state of existence that I have called the *Other Side* — now a very common term used by many people. These are facts backed up by evidence, actual research based on many years investigations and many sources and witnesses, not on faith or beliefs. I am not at all against people having faith, it stimulates their psychic response and thus their ability to receive contacts from the *Other Side*. But belief or disbelief produces information not based on facts, but on faith, or religion — and does not require any kind of objective confirmation. Proof lies in evidence obtained from many sources not connected with each other in any way.

All living entities, whether human, animal or plant, have within their visible outer body (or structure) a duplicate inner body that is contained in the being at the time birth occurs. It is the seal of the animal, the soul, with all its functions — memory, reasoning, feelings, etc. — and at the time of "death," only this outer body is dissolved while the inner body is untouched and moves into the spiritual dimension that is right around our physical world. Not up or down, but around it.

Since all faculties had been in this inner body, called the aura or soul, or etheric body, and since the spiritual dimension is made up of the same identical particles, the person (or animal, or plant) is right at home, so to speak, and perceives the spiritual world just as real and three-dimensional as the physical world. Everyone who have gone to the *Other Side* and communicated through reputable mediums about their lives over there, has made the same statement: the world they are now in is as real, as tangible to them as the one they have left behind.

If this sounds incredible, consider this. In our physical, three-dimensional world, we are solid, tangible, as is everything around us, like trees, houses, etc. — everything we can see or touch has a "body." That is because we also are three dimensional and have a body, so we are in the same dimension as are the objects or people we perceive. Now when you are in the spirit world, you are still made up of substance, only the particles that make up your substance, which are the same as everything around you, moves at a faster pace than the physical world, and everything in it. The physical world also consists of particles — the only difference between the two dimensions is the rate of speed.

For that logical reason, when a person from the physical, slower moving world wants to enter the faster moving spirit world, that is possible only if your etheric body does the moving — either through astral projection (if you are capable of doing it) or more likely with the help of a trance medium whose etheric (inner) body does all the traveling while the medium's physical self never leaves home, but reports all that he or she perceives or hears.

On the other hand, if a person living in the spirit world wants to visit the physical world, for whatever reason, such a person must slow down his or her vibrations (movement), and for that he or she also needs a trance medium on the physical plane, as a transformer. This process used to be called materialsation and resulted in a fully three dimensional appearance of the visitor, including touch, and if the visitor from the spirit world wanted to visit two-dimensionally, as it were, no medium as a transformer would have been necessary. What would have been required however, by the rules and regulations of the *Other Side*, permission from the Guide (superior) and a cause or reason that required such a visit, not to mention a lot of energy.

The *Other Side* of life is a very structured place indeed. It obeys certain scientific laws that are really only extensions of our own "ordinary" physical laws — extensions to accommodate a different but very natural dimension existing concentrically with our earth, our three dimensional world, but never clashing with it because the rate of movement is different. It's sort of like a polaroid light and an ordinary light occupying the same spacial area yet co-existing without clashing.

Everything that exists in the spirit world is created by someone's thoughts. Thoughts are energy, electromagnetic energy, to be exact. In the physical world, your thoughts can only become tangible if you record them on tape, write them down on paper, or put an image speaking these thoughts on film, video or tape. But once you have done so, it will stay recorded, and if you want to do away with those thoughts, you will have to destroy the paper or tape. In the spirit world, your thoughts instantly become tangible, a three dimensional reality (to you, as long as you are in the spirit world). If you want to undo these thoughts you will have to have new thoughts doing just that. Otherwise your thought creations do not fade by themselves and continue to be tangible in terms of the spirit world, forever.

If a visitor from the physical world, from our Earth for instance, visits the spirit world temporarily through astral travel or such events as near death experiences, everything that visitor sees, hears, and touches will be to him or her as it were occurring on our physical, three dimensional earth plane. In other words, nothing in this universe is intangible; both the physical world and the spirit world are tangible but to different degrees.

The question arises immediately, is there no difference at all between the two worlds? Of course there is.

To begin with, the notion of time and time factors are a necessary ingredient in the physical world, but not in the faster moving spirit world. Time in that dimension is measured in terms of states, situations, and accomplishments, not exact dates like days, weeks, and years. But when a communication occurs between the two dimensions then the *Other Side*'s operator will "translate" their non-time into our conventional time as best as possible.

This is so because the spirit world does not partake in our physical universe either: no sunrise, sunsets, or moon by which the Earth basically runs its schedules.

Because the spirit world is essentially an "eternal now," those who have passed into it usually appear younger and healthier (more desirable) than at the moment of passing. This is not surprising since the majority of people leave the physical world when their outer, physical bodies have deteriorated, having used up their allowed span of life. The only exceptions are cases where a person alive on the *Other Side* wishes to be recognized by loved ones, and prefers to show himself or herself as they looked later in life. But having made the contact and accomplished the desired recognition, they will immediately revert to the appearance of health and younger years they would normally prefer on the *Other Side*. This is entirely in their power and is also their decision, accomplished purely by thought — visualization of what they would like their appearance to be, or as they remember themselves most favorably. Thoughts are action over there, remember!

In the book I co-authored with Philip Solomon, his trance sessions also describe in full detail what the people in the spirit world do, what they can do, what they would want to do. Nobody sits around on clouds, playing the harp. On the *Other Side*, it seems, everybody lives a full and usually happy life based on what they did before coming here and following their own wishes. Nothing is impossible there if they can think of it. Now this should not be confused with our thinking of something in the physical life — it is still just a thought in our head and nothing more. If you walk onto a TV set and someone watches you on television, on their TV set you are flat, two-dimensional. But someone who has gone to the studio and watches the broadcast of the same scene, you and everyone else in the studio appear three-dimensional. The sound and the voices are the same because sound travels the same whether it is a thought world or a physical world, as long as there is air to carry it.

Those who have died and gone to the *Other Side* find that it is a very well organized world. There are organized concerts, games, activities, pretty much as on the physical side of life. People are free to associate with who they want to. From the moment of "passing over," there are people that take on the responsibility of helping the arrival get used to the new environment they have come to. With fewer exceptions than seems reasonable, people who die expecting eternal rest find instead a continuance of life with much of the earth life still having meaning there. Only those who have passed over with severe illnesses requiring heavy drugging, will at first be sent to hospitals, which are over there too, and now appear to the newcomer just as solid as those on earth. There they will be detoxified and after a while are able to pick up the life that was interrupted by the demise of their physical outer bodies.

Because relatively few people know what to expect after death, the initial emphasis is on explaining the *Other Side* to them. Some of the blame for this ignorance or misconceptions of what to expect, or to expect any kind of consciousness, must be placed on some aspects of organized religions that teach a merit system based on prayer and observance of rituals and in conformity with the various bibles. When none of these things occur there is a sense of surprise, and the realization that organized religion is after all man's interpretation of what he thinks is the Divine will, or what his priest or minister or rabbi has been telling him. What he gets instead is a life much closer to his life on earth, minus the need to fear illness or death, reunion with those who have "died" before him and are well and happy now, and a world not of tombstones and grief, but of life and health and joy.

Man soon learns that there is a choice, once he is accustomed to his new environment and world. He can stay, or if he prefers, register — yes, register — to go back into the incarnation cycle. The choice to do so is all his, but the selection of the new parents is in the hands of the folks who are running the *Other Side* so efficiently. To be sure, they are all people like the one who has just passed across the curtain, they have assignments according to their abilities and wishes, and the system works well indeed. There are no exceptions from it, the law is the law for everyone. When we pray to God, or to one of his special people such as saints or angels as we would call them, we really are asking for a special deal, an exception for us to obtain certain favors. But the *Other Side* is not likely to grant favors unless its directorate deems your request to be worthy of being granted — that also being part of the universal law, and there is a firmly established system in which both those in the spirit world and in the physical world participate.

I should emphasize that the choice of religion has absolutely nothing to do with the way the system works. In fact, there is a more direct way to reach out to the Deity than by delegating an intermediary, a priest, minister, or rabbi, or for that matter anyone else on earth, to represent you and your quest. You can do it yourself, and perhaps better, once you understand and accept the way the system works.

The *Other Side*, the spirit world, is a two-dimensional world only from our three-dimensional point of view, but to those who live in the spirit world, it is as three-dimensional as our physical world. That's because, in the physical world, thoughts are not visible or tangible, yet in the other world, they are both. Nearly everything can be similar between the two dimensions, with some adjustments — I don't want to say, differences, because in essence these are only adjustments to life in a world that functions differently from the one we may have left behind. On the positive side, there is the absence of illness and pain, there is the appearance as you were in your best, most desirable years, and there is absolutely no difficulty doing whatever it is you like doing.

If you are on a level — and of the levels more anon — where your comfort requires food and drink, and sleep, and day and night, all of these things will be yours the moment your thoughts create them in your mind. This is no hypnosis or suggestion: they are really created and become three-dimensional to you instantly over there. As you rise and develop to higher levels of the *Other Side*, you may not feel the need for these earthly elements and they will be gone as your thoughts adjust to their absence.

As far as sex is concerned, and this is a question frequently asked of me, the absence of a physically functioning body or denser matter makes sexual intercourse as it was impossible, but replaces it with something even more pleasurable. That is the blending of two individuals who wish to express their love and desire for each other, as their spirit bodies merge for that purpose.

As they rise to higher levels of the system, they may find the need for clothes unnecessary and replace them with a light, usually white "spirit robe" though they may go naked if they so desire. All in all, the spirit world, the *Other Side*, is a totally workable environment, consisting of several levels, with specific purposes and character. But it is neither heaven or hell as described by conventional religion.

The two halves — the spirit world and the physical world — are in contact with each other all the time, even though "time" as we know it on Earth does not exist on the *Other Side*; instead of "time," there are "states" of being ... beginnings and endings of certain actions. Though when dealing with the physical world, those in charge can adjust their actions and contacts to make sense in terms of our time on earth.

Contacts between people living in the physical world and those who live on the *Other Side* are always initiated by those on the *Other Side*, and they need to have the co-operation and permission of their individual spirit guides to make the contact, to reach out to those on the physical plane of existence. Unfortunately, many people still try to initiate the contact with loved ones or friends on the *Other Side* from their end, which can lead to frustration, or dealing with charlatans. But requesting such a contact in a specific manner (one that I will explain shortly), will make it possible, because the guides will then facilitate the connection as part of the system I have gotten to know as the best and surest way to make contacts possible — as part of the intervention system.

Lastly, spirits who are emotionally disturbed, earth-bound individuals popularly called ghosts, are really not part of the *Other Side* as yet; they are in the physical world, but not part of it, so they cannot therefore use the system of communication between the two worlds until they have moved across to the *Other Side*. Usually, they can only express themselves to physical beings with the help of and through trance mediums. In most cases, when that occurs, a skilled researcher will free them from their emotional turmoil and allow them to pass across to the *Other Side*.

Assuming that you, dear reader, are a balanced, rational individual, and that you are curious about the structure of that *Other Side* I am speaking of, I will not ask you to accept any of what I say on faith or belief. You are entitled to reasonable evidence — reasonable from a scientific point of view. Disbelief is as bad as uncritical belief, and faith is a sense of positive encouragement, but it's not equivalent to scientific evidence.

Strange as it seems, the knowledge of the exact structure of the *Other Side* is hardly recent. Emanuel Swedenborg, a Swedish medium and author, delineated it in precise terms in his work *Heaven and Hell*. Now there is neither one of these places in concrete terms, and Swedenborg used these terms only to dissociate himself from these religious concepts.

What there is, however, and the evidence for this can be found in the annals of physical research, not organized religion, is indeed the *Other Side* of life, which is also part of life as we know it. Based on my studies of many years and research and numerous trance sessions, both by myself with various deep trance mediums, and the work of medium Philip Solomon, with whom I co-authored a new book titled *Beyond Death*, there is a well defined system of seven levels of existence, once we cross from the physical world into the Spirit world.

• Level One is very much like our earth, and all our weaknesses and evils are still with those who had these afflictions prior to the dissolution of the physical body, continuing their aspect of life very much as before. Here we might find those who have committed crimes, often unrepenting, but the majority of human beings arrive on Level Two, which does not harbor the evil of Level One.

• Level Two does allow the new arrival to have much of what they had been used to in the physical world.

They are now taken in hand by loved ones who had come over before, and those in need of healing because of the nature of their deaths, would be taken to hospital facilities for a short time.

• Level Three allows further development, while still accommodating what the arrivals had known on the physical plane; but it's not directed toward a better understanding of the spiritual nature of man and the expression thereof.

• By Level Four the need for earth type clothing gives way to a flowing white gown, called The Spirit Robe, but individuality remains and helping those on the physical world is now an aim and can be facilitated with the help of the guides. Rising from one level to the next is difficult for those who are not ready for the transition, and if tried without help and approval from the guides, will result in difficulties with your breathing and orientation.

• Level Five will harbor the spiritual leaders, and is where those who are potential guides in the future come. Physical appetites such as food and sex have now disappeared or been relegated to positions of little interest.

• Level Six is the seat of government, so to speak. It is here we would encounter (if we did) the "Board of Directors" who are the actual governing body of the universe — both Spiritual and Physical. They are highly developed, enlightened individuals, but at one time they too were human beings. There are no living entities on the *Other Side* who were not human beings at one point in their ascent, contrary of fanciful stories about heavenly beings. They have been observed as, and been referred to, as "Beings of Light." In many reported accounts of near death experiences, the individual encounters a "Being of Light" at the end of the long tunnel leading from the physical world to the World of Spirit. These "Beings of Light" are much more than guides. Guides carry out the laws of the *Other Side*; "Beings of Light" create those laws.

P.M.H. Atwater, the celebrated author who has written extensively about the Near Death Experience — which she herself went through — calls the assembly of the Beings of Light the Circle of Light. They are the council at the top of the sixth level that encompasses the spirit world.

What then of the Seventh Level? As it is described by the Beings of Light, that is where the Godhead — the Light itself — is situated. They speak of it only as a powerful source of light. Miss Atwater tells me that "a number of both adults and children have spoken of this council as Beings of Light."

Finally, amongst the large number of deep trance sessions that Medium Philip Solomon has conducted, and are recorded in our book *Beyond Death*, there is one particularly telling session with an entity who calls himself Michael. He informs us that there are indeed seven levels to the *Other Side*, and that the Circle of Light has presently nine members; there had been a tenth one in the past, of which Michael does not wish to speak.

But numbers are terribly important as the keys to the universe, and I decided to research the number of Beings of Light in the "circle" even further. In our solar system, we have nine bodies; Sun, Moon, Jupiter, Neptune, Uranus, Mars, Venus, Mercury, Earth and Pluto. Was there a tenth Being of Light also? Is he the legendary Fallen Angel? Michael is being questioned: Is he an angel? Michael hesitates before he answers, and then, reluctantly, agrees he is.

Angelos means messenger in Greek.

"Beings of Light," or angels, these nine individuals are as high up as can be. Beyond them, pure energy, divine power? Nirvana?

The individuals have blended into a group, as well, on the Sixth Level.

Those are the facts.

Chapter Seven:
How the *Other Side* Intervenes in Our Lives

> *Most importantly, how do the people on the Other Side intervene in our lives? How does it work?*

T here seems to be two directions in which the inter-play between the spiritual world and the physical world takes place.

One is, the influence (leading to action) that is initiated wholly by the "personnel" on the *Other Side* of life. The way the system works is that every one of us in the physical world represents a kind of investment in the overall plan. Nothing is accidental or haphazard in either universe. The personnel I just referred to are of course people who have passed over and continue to live an orderly existence in the other dimension until they decide to go back into the physical world again through reincarnation. But while they are active over there, they don't sit around idly on 'cloud 9,' stroking their wings or playing the harp. Only in movies and religious fantasy do they do that sort of thing, and of course such people simply do not exist in reality.

Each and every person coming over to the *Other Side* is given a task according to their abilities and to some degree, preferences. Everybody works. The next dimension is not a welfare state. Their task is to keep an eye on certain people, not on everybody perhaps, but on those where the system's investment is considerable. By investment, I mean the gift of intelligence, personality, a good spiritual body and a matching physical body, all nicely planned when the moment to re-enter the physical world arrives.

The spiritual law requires those who are given particular abilities to use them constructively and actively. If they do not, or ignore their "inner voice" messages, emanating of course from the folks on the *Other Side*, they not only disappoint their handlers, but themselves as such inaction will automatically result in a lower karmic balance next time around.

But there is one problem with this interaction between the personnel on the *Other Side* trying to monitor, counsel, and steer their physical clients assigned to them by the system based on mutual bonds of knowledge and skills between the living person on earth and the guiding person on the *Other Side*. They can nudge, they can send messages via the "inner voice" (call it V-mail, if you like), and if all else fails, maybe communicate through a psychic or medium, or maybe directly in the dream state. But they cannot do the job for their client on earth. The client, the person in the physical world, gets only the hint and the opportunity, not the outcome. That is the client's own contribution to the (end) result. There is a fine line, I have been told many times in communication sessions, where intervention ends because it would violate the natural law. No miracles, please. No suspension of reality in the physical world. Close to it, if you wish, yes, but not beyond that line. We, too, have a sacred obligation to fully utilize our abilities, talents, and gifts to the fullest extent. That is why the spiritual system can only go so far. Usually, that is far enough.

That which people without understanding of the spiritual world call "coincidence" or "accidental" or the result, somehow, of one's own maneuverings, is of course not that at all. But it has to look like it at times, to cover up any hint of outside intervention. Once you understand this and act accordingly, the relationship between yourself and your mentor or mentors will run smoothly.

There are no "coincidences" in the physical universe, despite a popular concept to explain "seemingly" connected situations. Such a view reflects pure materialistic, rational thinking, totally ignoring the fact that our physical world is a highly complex system, hardly the kind that allows such sloppy goings-on as "coincidence" or "accidents." Even the great psychiatrist Carl Jung knew this when he postulated his system of "meaningful coincidence" between events, which he termed the law of acausal synchronicity.

When we speak of cause and effect, we ordinarily stay within the boundaries of common events with which we are familiar. But cause and effect can hardly fit extraordinary events and situations that we do not even fully comprehend, such as earth changes, space discoveries, and to some extent, our weather patterns.

Even more than in the physical world, coincidences and meaningless connections between events are unthinkable in the spiritual dimension, where thought and mental communication are important, and very real instruments of the system. Putting aside for the moment the question of origin—Divine or otherwise—this is a highly sophisticated system and as it pervades all of our aspects of life, in so effective and meaningful a manner, it is not likely to have left its homework undone, so to speak, and allowed irregularities not under its control to exist. In fact, they don't.

We are all part of this system, for better or worse, and we don't have any choice in this matter since it is the very essence of what we are: physical as well as spiritual beings. Edgar Cayce, dubbed "the sleeping prophet," has stated that "the body is not structural, but functional," meaning that the spiritual inner body, seat of the persona, "manifests" the outer, physical body, and the two work together in unison. Most medical men will insist that the body is structural and that mind is somehow part of the central nervous system. Never mind the etheric body or the persona!

There are two kinds of intervention: 1. Action initiated by the *Other Side* without our knowledge or request, but to our benefit in some manner, and of course carefully monitored by "them." 2. Action requested by us, for help or guidance.

Both of these types of intervention require certain conditions:

1) The recipient or supplicant must have reached a full understanding of the spiritual nature of man, and live accordingly.

2) In the case of unrequested action by the *Other Side* on our behalf, we ourselves have not been able to initiate such action either because we do not know the possibilities awaiting us, or because we have tried, yet failed to achieve certain goals.

In each case, of course, the goal must be spiritually positive, and not of a destructive or harmful nature.

3) As supplicant, we must use the kind of direct appeal that gets results. This is not an ordinary prayer, nor will you find it printed in any of your bibles or other religious books. But this is the "formula" that will get results! I have tried these past years to lead my life in balance and harmony, and of course according to the spiritual guidelines I have outlined.

It is important to realize that the *Other Side* never wastes any effort. If an intervention, or only a hint, or nudge comes your way, there must be a good reason for it, even though you may not recognize it. But you must follow through, regardless, or you are the loser.

I should point out that all individuals are just that, different in many ways, and not numbers; we may have been "created" equal, but we are certainly not equal in any sense. What the "system" (the combination of both the physical and spiritual systems) puts into each one of us is always unique and never a duplicate or a clone. Truly, each man or woman is a unique being, as, to a large extent, are animals, especially pets living with humans. Thus, our opportunities will differ widely according to the potential given us in this lifetime. The personnel of the *Other Side* is not so foolish as to try to make an untalented person into a piano wizard. To the contrary, they carefully shape their input into our lives to the potential within us to succeed!

I have no doubts whatsoever of the reality of this input, not on philosophical grounds, not even as the result of careful scientific inquiry into many cases, but on the grounds of solid, strictly personal experience. It was there all the time, but I failed to notice it until many years later. Perhaps that was as it should be, because I might not have been ready to fully comprehend the system's workings at an earlier stage in my development.

In sharing with you, dear readers, what is essentially a personal occurrence, I do so for only one reason. This is not an ego-trip, to brag about my good fortunes in having the *Other Side* look after me so well, maybe because I am such a valuable "investment" on their part. I divulge the amazing events in my life that have convinced me that this intervention does, in fact exist, and exist for most of us in various degrees and manners, because if it convinced me, it should at least convince you to consider the matter seriously in respect to your own life. After all, you are still in charge of your reactions, and have free will.

Long before I was aware of the spiritual system I know now, there was an incident that is meaningful only in retrospect. Clearly the *Other Side* was interested in my work in this field. I know this now and have for some time. But in 1966, I had no such notion. My former wife Catherine and I were in Freiburg in Germany for a lecture I delivered at the community college on "life after death" evidence. Afterwards, we were walking through the old city, which was pretty dark by now. In deep thought, I was about to cross a narrow street, when Catherine, on a strange and sudden impulse, yanked me back. A second later, a speeding car raced by me. I would have surely been killed instantly if she had not so acted. Catherine had no idea what made her do it, but I am glad she did!

While we still had our summer house in the Austrian Alps, at Bad Aussee, we were having lunch in the kitchen, which was a large, modern, up-to-date eat-in kitchen with a tile floor. My younger daughter, Alexandra, was just a little baby in 1972 when this happened. She was seated in a highchair as babies of about a year usually are when, suddenly, she began to sway in her chair and the chair was about to fall over backwards. Her head would have hit the tile floor from a considerable height, and the results could have been fatal. As I looked on in paralyzed horror, and as the chair reached a "point of no return" midway between normal and floor, an unseen hand pushed it back to its proper position, and the baby did not keel over. At the time of the seeming miracle I thought that the definitely friendly ghost of an earlier owner of the old house had intervened, but now I am not so sure; was it the old farmer's wife, or was it a more direct hand from the *Other Side*?

When the *Other Side* desires that I meet certain people, because they can see ahead what might develop between us of a positive nature — that is, if I responded properly —they will sometimes go to great lengths to make the link.

In 1992, I was "impressed" to pick up a section of the *Sunday Times* that I rarely look at, because I am not exactly in the market for a position. That particular day, however, my eye fell upon a small ad requesting assistance with the writing of the autobiography of a psychic healer. I thought I should at least contact these people and see how I could help them, even though they wanted a "ghost writer," and while I write about ghosts, I am not a ghost writer.

From this meeting grew a long-term relationship and friendship with Ze'ev Kolman. The book has since become a book about the healer, not an autobiography. What was particularly intriguing to me, in retrospect now, is that the *Other Side* knew exactly whom they wanted to write this book. Of course "they" did not tell me right out. I brought a dear friend into the picture, an experienced journalist, to do the job, because I felt I was too much committed to psychic healing, and of course a more neutral writer might be better. But I was wrong. It turned out my friend had to withdraw from the project and I was asked by the healer to undertake the job, which I did. It was clear to him, and, by then, to me too, that I really was the right man for the job.

This of course presupposes that the folks *Over There* keep a close tab on me: and they do. They also do the same for you, if you are someone who warrants their care, for whatever reason. The value system in the spiritual dimension is very firm: all human beings are not worth monitoring and helping, but many are. It is a little like the fellows in charge of scholarships: they will hand them out to the best candidates, and many won't get any. Our world is a world of merit and achievement.

Some years back I had some unsuccessful dealings with a man named Jim, from India, who promised a lot and delivered nothing. But he was a charmer and I never regretted the experience. For several years he disappeared completely. One fine day I tried to catch a certain bus on the corner of Fifth Avenue and Eighth Street in New York, a bus that does not run too frequently. As I approached the bus, the driver, no doubt with a sense of glee (for he had seen me), pulled out and left me standing there. I let out a low-level curse, when I heard someone laugh behind me. It turned out to be Jim, who invited me for coffee. We spent a few minutes chatting, when he asked me about a mutual friend, Jerry. I replied I had not been in touch with him either for a long time.

We parted company shortly after, and I wondered why on earth we had met in such a peculiar way. Then I thought, why not call Jerry and tell him about it; he may be amused. When I reached Jerry, he informed me that he had been trying to get in touch with me for some time, because he had an exciting business proposition to discuss!

The *Other Side* clearly prevented me from catching that bus so I could run into Jim, so he could ask me about Jerry, so I would naturally tell Jerry. All perfectly natural and "normal." Or is it?

Sometimes the "stage managing" really goes to extremes, and I admire the folks on the *Other Side* for their consummate skills in doing it.

During the last few years I have had very few college lectures, perhaps because money for fees is hard to come by. Then a group at the Westchester Community College invited me to speak about scientific evidence for life after death, one of my most popular illustrated talks. That was in February of 1993. In early March, I was informed that the school would not approve the expenditure, and regretfully, they had to withdraw the invitation.

But then something strange happened. Within two weeks, they called me back. Evidently, the board had reversed itself and now the lecture could go on after all, in April of 1993. And so it did. But that is only a small part of the story.

The week before the scheduled lecture, the college ran an announcement of it for the general public on a local Westchester cable channel. At the exact time the announcement was going to run, a young woman by the name of Marisa, who had been psychic all her life, somehow was "made" to turn on the channel, which she ordinarily never watches. At this precise moment, the announcement of my lecture came on, and Marisa decided to attend.

After the lecture, she came over and introduced herself, and mentioned something about writing science-fiction, and a deep interest in the psychic world. She handed me her card, which I put on my desk and went on to other matters. But the next day I felt strangely compelled to call her and invite her to see me. It was then that I discovered that perhaps her science-fiction, about which she was thinking of consulting me, was not really the reason we met. I encouraged her to become a professional psychic, and she did.

Today she is one of the most successful psychic readers in her part of the world, and a close friend. I helped her develop her gift further, and to make the transition from being a volunteer to a professional, making a living being of service to many people in need of just that.

The long arm of intervention by the *Other Side* can evidently plan things way ahead, being able to see developments — possible developments, that is — in our time continuum from their world where there is no time as we here know it.

A psychically talented woman from Queens, New York, had led a very difficult life: broken marriages, children, and problems all around. Apparently, the *Other Side* had kept an eye on her all along and decided to help her do what she did best — be a fine medium. But first things were financially so bad, she took on a job as a housekeeper for a married lady in New York. The lady happened to be a good friend of mine, and one day she

called me to acquaint me with the amazing psychic predictions by this woman, that had come true, suggesting
that I investigate her.

That was twenty-five years ago. I met the woman,
started to work with her, test her, monitor her work,
and before long she set up on her own as a professional
psychic reader and medium. The late Yolana Lassaw was
probably the premier medium in America, with clients
sometimes having to wait weeks before they can be seen;
she has worked successfully with police in solving cases
and with me in cases of possession, and other complicated situations. All this, I am sure, was stage-managed
by the *Other Side*.

Now and then, trifling things happen that seem also
due to deliberate intervention. I was trying to hurry home
on a particularly hot afternoon recently, and reached the
bus stop just as the bus I was to take pulled out, ignoring me completely. Before I could utter a nasty word,
an express bus going in the same direction pulled up. I
was home in half the time it would have taken me on
the other bus.

My former mother-in-law suddenly needed a serious
operation for a brain tumor earlier this year. As she often
stays at my place when she comes to Manhattan, I immediately made inquiries as to who was the best surgeon
for this kind of operation. A good friend, an experienced
journalist who had written medical stories and even a

book about two doctors with unusual ideas, suggested a surgeon she felt was the best man for the job.

I arranged for my mother-in-law to see my personal physician, Dr. Karl Goodman, a man I respected for his wide knowledge and also his open-mindedness in medicine and alternative cures. I briefly mentioned the name of the surgeon my journalistic friend had suggested, but Dr. Goodman did not know him. Instead, he suggested someone he knew extremely well, and when he did, I just knew this was the right man, and not the other doctor. The operation was a complete success.

When necessary, the "operators" on the *Other Side* do not hesitate to intervene with physical objects as if "by unseen hands."

A few years back, I was in Hollywood seeing various people in respect to my film and television interests. I received an invitation from a good friend of mine, an actress, to attend a party in Truncas, which is way below Malibu and quite a distance from Hollywood. My friend, whom I was seeing at the time, came along and drove her car. Now this car was in rather bad shape and needed repair. In the daytime, there was no problem, but in the dark, there would be a problem, she advised me, because the light on the left side of the car had been knocked out and only the one on the right was working. Just the same we went to the party, and by the time we returned to Hollywood, it was already dark.

We drove along the Pacific Highway in an area where there were absolutely no street lights, and all we had was that one light on the right side of the car. Not only was this illegal, it was highly dangerous as another car coming up behind us would not be able to judge our position, nor could a car coming in the opposite direction. As we both individually worried about it, a strange thing occurred. I noticed it first. The light on the left side was also on! Now there was no way this could be and no reflection to account for it, but clearly, two strong beams were visible in front of us. After a while, my friend whispered, "Do you see what I see?" I replied, "You mean the left light?" She nodded and I confirmed that I, too, was aware of it being there. We said nothing more as we drove through the dark landscape. Then we reached the point on the highway where the street lights of Malibu begin. Instantly, the mysterious left light disappeared. We stopped the car and looked at it. All that was there was a gaping hole. No bulb. No wires. No light.

Now I don't know how "they" do those things, but they do.

Chapter Eight:

Following That "Inner Voice"

*How to follow that "Inner Voice"; it gives
you excellent directions. Just listen.*

T he second manner in which the *Other Side* influences us I have come to call the Inner Voice, which
is a pretty good description of its mechanics. The
skeptic may say that it is merely a thought of your own,
which just comes to you, and you follow through or not.
Not so, however, because the true Inner Voice is quite
different from thoughts that originate within you.

One's own thoughts are generally slow moving,
sometimes even hesitating, while you're considering
them. They are not particularly startling or sudden or all
that compelling, and oftentimes one tends to ignore one's
own thoughts especially when they are not connected
with the thought process pertaining to what you are doing at the time. Random thoughts are usually dismissed
an unimportant, and many are.

But the Inner Voice is much more like an intruding broadcast, demanding to be listened to. The Inner Voice is a silent but extremely sharp and precise message to you, a message that can run the gamut from dire warning to positive suggestion. Now some will call that intuition, and it is a moot question whether you believe the voice is only an extension of your unconscious, or of external origin. From my own experience I am quite sure that what we call intuition is rarely of our own making, but almost always the work of the folks on the *Other Side*, letting us know something that will benefit us. While they are not really looking for "credit" for doing it, they deserve it.

Why then would the *Other Side* use the direct intervention at times, and the Inner Voice communication at others? I think it has to do with the value system of the spiritual world. When the Inner Voice is used to give us hints, or warnings, it is necessary for us to take steps to heed the voice. We do have free will and can ignore it, usually to our detriment. That choice however, and the action we take upon being aware of the Inner Voice message, is important. Remember, the relationship between the spiritual system and us in the physical world is not a one-way street. Our cooperation and reaction to what we are given is very much a part of the outcome.

The Inner Voice should never be ignored: the folks on the *Other Side* don't waste energy and would not bother to contact us if it were not important for us. Unfortunately, the majority of people tend to take the Inner Voice far from seriously, if they even acknowledge its existence. But then the spiritual way may not yet be for everyone.

One of the difficulties, at times, is the apparent conflict between what the Inner Voice counsels, and pure logic. Most people, unfortunately, still go by logical reasoning and find comfort in it, ignoring the Inner Voice. Usually they realize their mistake later, when the matter touched upon by the Inner Voice has come to pass.

The Inner Voice is a direct line to the *Other Side*. But the system does not allow the personnel over there to influence or help you indiscriminately. Far from it. Every message transmitted through the channel of the Inner Voice must conform to the spiritual law as it pertains to you. Individuality is very important, as we are all different as is our actions, based on the evaluation process by which we are being given counsel through the Inner Voice.

The Inner Voice does not announce itself to get your attention. It is a sudden, often "gnawing" thought, very specific and direct, about something you ought to do, or not do. Sometimes it feels like a hunch, sometimes like a vague sense of discomfort about some situation you are about to enter, but enough specifics are always involved so that you know what the Inner Voice is trying to tell you.

Don't ignore those signs: "they" know more than you do about your life and what is coming up for you. I realize that this involves absolute faith in the accuracy of the message: but you will never have a working relationship with the *Other Side* unless you can demonstrate that faith.

Sometimes the Inner Voice deals with relatively small matters, though not minor to you at the time.

How do I know all this? From personal experience.

Once, I had a foreign body in my eye, and it troubled me greatly. I knew it needed to be removed quickly or it would cause even more problems. But this was Sunday afternoon, and we all know that weekends is no time to get sick if you want a doctor. To go to an emergency clinic gives me the willies, knowing how I would have to wait for hours just to be seen.

Suddenly, the Inner Voice said loud and clear, though of course silently, "go see your eye doctor, he will be there." I responded, silently also, "but it is Sunday afternoon." Nevertheless, I raced to his office. Sure enough he was there, having come in to deal with some personal business.

I was traveling from Munich to London, and routinely went through the passport control on my way to board the plane. I then discovered to my horror, that my passport was in another jacket, and that other jacket was inside my luggage, which I had checked earlier and which, by now, was aboard the plane! What to do? Bravely, I spoke with the German officer, and he was kind enough to let me go aboard; after all, I had the ticket. But he also warned me that his British colleagues might not be as accommodating and I was taking a chance.

I arrived in London, and with some trepidation, went toward the bank of passport control officers facing arriving passengers. Suddenly, I heard the Inner Voice "direct" me to a particular officer, a young woman. I followed through, she was sympathetic and allowed me to get my luggage, take out the passport, and then have it stamped. She did not have to do that, but she did.

Some years ago, I found myself without a new book contract, and I began to worry about securing more income. Then a strange train of thought entered my mind, how about re-issuing some of your successful out-of-print books? How, I replied, and I realized the suggestion came from the Inner Voice. Write a letter, the voice commanded, write a letter! No sooner heard, then done. I sat down and wrote not one, but two identical letters to the presidents of both Waldenbooks and Barnes & Noble, telling them what they were missing by not re-issuing my old books. Both responded quickly, and their editors offered me contract after contract, republishing many of my long out-of-print books, brought up to date and nicely produced.

I was visiting the cemetery where our old cook, Anna, who had helped bring me up for eighteen years, was buried. I had been there the year before and never found her grave. This time, I insisted, I would have to find it. I asked the cemetery people, but Anna died many years ago, and they could not help me. It got late, and my companion wanted to get back to Vienna. In desperation, I closed my eyes, to be more receptive, and sure enough, the Inner Voice told me to go down this row, then turn right to the end of the next one, and down again to the middle. Sure enough, there was her grave, and I was finally able to place some flowers on it, after all these years.

In 1979, a close friend of mine had a terrible automobile accident as the result of crossing a street in Hollywood after a violent argument with her then boyfriend. Her visitor's visa had also just expired, and only because of her injuries, she was given a three month extension, after which she would have to return to her native England.

I was very fond of the young lady, and wanted to help her so I telephoned a certain Senator and asked for help. Shortly afterwards, the Senator's secretary called back and informed me sadly, that there was no way my friend could stay in the United States. It would appear that on her previous application for a visa, in London, her boyfriend had insisted on being referred to as her fiancée, and that her purpose of coming to America was to marry him. Unfortunately, this ran afoul an old law, and caused my friend to be permanently excluded from coming here. Time went on and my friend's departure seemed almost certain. During my last conversation with her, by telephone between New York and Los Angeles, I suddenly "heard" myself say, "don't worry, I am going to get you a visa." I realized at once that I had just repeated what the Inner Voice had "told" me. She was delighted but incredulous; everybody she had consulted, from lawyers to the ambassador, had told her that her case was hopeless.

Well, I took my quest seriously. Armed with necessary papers, I requested an interview with the head of immigration in New York, using as reference the name of the head of the passport office, whom I happened to know. I was received most cordially. Once again, I felt the Inner Voice guiding me. Rather than come out with the purpose of my visit, I heard myself discussing the man's name and its origin — was it English or Swiss? He was thrilled at the idea that anyone cared, and we had a long discussion about family origins. Then I casually explained that I needed a so-called H-1 visa for a year for a young woman whom I wanted to work with me in research projects (which was true) and I handed him the forms I had prepared, which already had my friend's signature on the application. Now, an H-1 visa is usually only given to very unique people whose presence in America might contribute to our knowledge of some other benefit. Einstein originally had such a very special visa. Oh yes, the head of immigration said, "Debbie, take care of the professor," and with that his secretary casually processed the application. A week later my friend had her visa, and I was able to renew it for her three more times, three more years, after which she decided to return to England.

On the other hand, going against your Inner Voice's urging can have disastrous consequences at times. A friend forced me to join her in a lawsuit that really was without merit, but, because she had been helpful to me at times, I agreed. All this time my Inner Voice screamed at me, don't, don't! As a result of going against the voice; I became liable for court costs and had all kinds of problems, which I neither deserved nor needed.

Also, don't confuse the Inner Voice with prayer. The Inner Voice, just like direct intervention, originates with the *Other Side*, and it is they who decide when to contact you in this manner. However, your own input is vital for it to be successful, and you can ignore it, either accidentally, or out of fear or for some other reason. But if you listen, and I always listen, you can only derive benefits from the Inner Voice.

Chapter Nine

How to Get Help from the *"Other Side"*

> Forget about the old way of asking for help from the spirit world. This is the proven formula that is always answered. Just follow Dr. Holzer's exact instructions on how to proceed.

C learly, when the *Other Side* feels that intervention on their part is required — and the judgment is entirely that of the guides who run the "day to day" activities, the "government" on that side — they who are in charge will know exactly what to do to remedy a situation on this side, but in such a way that the universal law is not breeched, and that their intervention seems perfectly natural and in no way supernatural. No "Deus Ex Machina" as in the ancient Greek drama here: it all lies within the boundaries of what is rationally a possible event.

But I have long viewed these incursions into our world by those on the *Other Side*, incursions for our benefit, as a kind of investment being protected. It seems to me that certain people now living on the *Other Side* are charged with the careful and continual observation of those over here, especially those with specific talents that might benefit humanity and the world when properly used.

To be sure, not every person on this side of the curtain fits that description. Far from it, the number is limited, but when intervention occurs from the *Other Side*, it is mostly in respect to people with gifts that would benefit mankind, the world, and the spiritual way of life. Having given certain individuals certain talents, certain gifts, the guides on the *Other Side* consider them as a kind of investment that they want to watch carefully and, when necessary, protect by intervening. The individuals with gifts and abilities beyond average, beyond ordinary people's abilities, are the favored stock on this spiritual stock exchange, so to speak, and the guides are the players, leaving us nothing more than to acknowledge their help, and say thank you. For they have no trouble watching us, this side of life and acting as required to have these gifts and talents succeed, pay off as it were, in a positive way.

Those of us who understand the system will be aware of their intervention, but many who do not grasp the duality of the world will explain unexpected intervention or help as "accidental" or good fortunes. The guides do not care about that either because the results of what these individuals accomplish due to the unsought intervention are much more important to them and their plans than the individuals who are being helped. Thus, the majority of human beings is not even aware of the help coming their way, from the *Other Side*, unsought, but very important to their success.

But the number of individuals on this side needing help one way or the other is far greater than the number of outstanding individuals the *Other Side* watches and guides to best use of their gifts. Ordinary people who have needs and problems, who cannot solve them themselves, no matter how much they have tried, are of three kinds:

• There are the agnostics, who have no belief in the *Other Side* or even religion as a way to get help.

• The second group are those who believe that God and prayer will help. These range from vaguely religious people to those who pray to specific saints or to God or to Jesus, prayer being simply a way to express their needs and asking for help, sometimes very emotionally.

• Then there is the third group: people who acknowledge a High Power that they can call anything from God to The Light to Friends on the *Other Side*, keeping within their own belief system.

It is this third group, which includes this author, that has proven itself to be the most realistic and workable in the quest for help, and I am about to share with you, dear reader, how it works and why.

There is only one pre-condition to make it happen. You should either lead a life that conforms to the Spiritual Way of Life, or at least subscribe to it and, as you put forth your request for help, start living by its concepts henceforth. I have long lived by it, and the result was

years of help when needed, without exception: but usually that help forthcoming was in the form that helped
me most — not necessarily exactly as I had envisioned
it, and its timing was not always instantaneous but at the
right time and under the most appropriate conditions.

The *Other Side* will determine how to best respond,
both from the point of view of your needs, and what is
appropriate under the spiritual system and law. You want
help? You will get it, if you follow my suggestions. Some
years ago, I realized that the spiritual system was as real
as the physical world, and that the balance between the
two was what life should be like.

There was the time, years ago, when I found myself in
a sudden financial bind and decided to try to sell some of
my antiques. But times were not favorable in New York
for ordinary fine arts, and I failed to attract anyone interested. Twenty-four hours later, I received a telephone call
from a man who had just arrived on a visit to New York
from Venezuela, where he was a wealthy businessman.
He had found my name listed in the directory of the
Appraisers' Association as an authority on European art.
Could I look at an Icon his wife had recently acquired?
I agreed, and they came to my house where I told his
wife that the piece was just fine.

They were about to leave, when his wife caught a
glimpse of my collection of paintings and Icons. Some of
them I had kept when my wife, who is Russian-French,
and I divorced and she moved out. The majority I had

given to her and, of course I wanted her to have them, but the handful of those Icons that I still had immediately attracted the man's wife, and he insisted on buying them from me. It turned out that the sum involved was practically the amount I needed quickly at that time. Coincidence? Hardly. There are dozens of experts on European art listed in that directory. Why pick me? I had asked him that question. He did not really know, and he said, "it just came to me."

When my elder daughter, Nadine, was still in a private high school, she ran into difficulties with her grades. Eventually, it got to the point where she was threatened with expulsion if she could not perform at a level her headmaster, an Englishman who had studied at Oxford, considered the absolute minimum. I was asked to come to the school to hear the bad news. When I sat opposite the stern headmaster, it became immediately clear to me that he had already made up his mind, and I was to hear the verdict. At that moment, though, a thought impressed itself on my conscious mind, the word "tutor."

When the headmaster had finished telling me why Nadine should find another school to continue her studies, I spoke up quietly and pleaded with him to give her one more chance for the next term. I offered to hire a tutor, one of the staff of this school whom I knew, a lady who was very competent and on good terms with the headmaster. It all went by him, though, and he kept shaking his head, saying that it wouldn't do any good.

But suddenly, he stopped, and looked straight at me. "All right, one more term." We shook hands, I left, bathed in sweat, and Nadine continued her studies, did extremely well the next term, and graduated among the better students.

Sometimes the answer to my problem takes an enormous amount of maneuvering for the *Other Side* to get the desired results, and may involve several people, and specific circumstances in order to happen.

My younger daughter's fiancé had run into a problem with his car insurance and license. Under the pressure of changing jobs, changing apartments and planning his wedding, he had failed to renew both. Unfortunately, he was caught, and his license to drive was lifted. Since he then required a car to make a living, this was a virtual disaster for the young man, and what made the case nearly hopeless was the statutory provision that someone driving without valid insurance would automatically have his license suspended for a full year. That would be the end of his job, of course.

I offered to help, being a typical Aquarian and also the future father-in-law. I approached the governor and the police chief in the town where the matter took place, and got absolutely nowhere. The license bureau was of no help either. In my predicament, and with the court hearing coming up before long, I asked for help (from the Other Side). I explained that I had run out of avenues and needed intervention. While I was waiting, with complete faith, for answers, I contacted the prosecuting attorney who was to present the case in court. He was polite, but non-committal.

Once again, I spoke to the prosecutor, and it turned out that he was not on duty on the day of the hearing, after all, but another attorney would be. The new prosecutor seemed more sympathetic regarding the circumstances of the case, despite the fact that the law allowed no exceptions and the judge could not do a thing about it. But then I felt a warmth enveloping me, and I became very relaxed.

"Look," I said, "the officer asked him to produce proof of his insurance. He did not have it." All the other "problems" having been straightened out, it had really boiled down to this point.

"I see," the prosecutor said. "Of course you realize it all depends on the police officer who stopped the young man."

Meanwhile, a local attorney, an old court hand, had been retained by the family. He had told them from the outset that the suspension of the license for a year was not negotiable, but perhaps the other "problem," the missed license renewal, could be dealt with simultaneously, not in addition. That was the extent of his prognosis. When I offered to help by appearing at the hearing, he curtly told me not to interfere. The day came for the hearing, and the young man went bravely, expecting his license to be suspended for a full year. Picture his surprise when the police officer stated truthfully that he could not produce a valid insurance. On that basis, he received a month's suspension, and twenty-eight days later he was again driving to work.

Coincidence? Hardly.

Intervention in emergency situations, even in hopeless circumstances, is never ignored if you do it right. I was trying to get home from a friend's New Year's Eve party several years ago. To my horror I soon discovered that the buses were not running, and taxis either would not stop at all or were already engaged. To make matters worse, it had begun to rain and there I stood shivering at the corner of Sixth Avenue and 14th Street in New York, waiting to find some kind of transportation to get home uptown. The minutes passed, I had been standing there for over an hour and was becoming really worried. Images of having to sleep in the street or go to a hotel began to emerge in my mind. Then I asked for INTERVENTION. Suddenly, I felt a warmth, and I got the impression I should go around the corner to 14th Street. I replied, in my mind, that I had been there before several times, and nothing had happened, no taxi, no bus.

I nevertheless decided to do it, and went around the corner to 14th Street. I stood there for another ten minutes, shivering, and growing more and more miserable. Suddenly, a cab, with occupants inside, stopped right in front of me. I hesitated for a moment, seeing it was an occupied vehicle. Then the door opened, and one person got out. I raced to the cab and asked if they had room for me. They asked, where was I going? It turned out I was going only a few blocks from their destination. They invited me to hop in, and I got home safely. Coincidence? Not likely.

Does lightening ever strike twice? Only when the folks on the *Other Side* want it to.

Having nearly forgotten my harrowing New Year's Eve experience of being marooned in a storm the year before, I confidently went to my friend's apartment again on New Year's Eve. At 1:30 a.m. I left and tried to get home. Tried is the word. There wouldn't be any buses for the next hour and a half, I discovered. There were plenty of cabs, but all were full and racing by me in a show of supreme disregard for my plight.

"Not again" I thought in dismay, and as time went by and I began to feel uneasy about getting home, the memory of last year's amazing rescue came to mind. I am stuck, I've tried everything to no avail, I said silently, Intervention please!

Around me dozens of equally stranded people were waving frantically at passing taxis — all occupied. I looked down the street into the distance, which was easier this year as the night was dry and clear. But no taxi light shone in the distance; nothing was coming my way... Suddenly, out of nowhere, a cab stopped just in front of me, lights on and impossibly, yet obviously, available. I grabbed the door and got in as those around me looked on in amazement, and, I suspect, resentment. Fifteen minutes later I was home. Now I did not see this cab coming down the street, and I have 20/20 vision. But I thanked the "upstairs department" for having rescued me, once again, reinforcing my firm understanding of the system and what it takes to have your prayer answered.

Not all situations for which I sought relief were crises, or truly threatening, but they were problems or situations that caused me difficulty or great unhappiness, and I had no further avenues available to change them.

Years ago, when I was promoting my books in Los Angeles, I was booked on many television and radio programs, sometimes at close intervals. It was crucial to be on time. Unfortunately, I do not drive a car, and had to rely on taxi cabs. More than once I found myself marooned at the last interview site, waiting for a cab to arrive to take me to the next appointment. But Los Angeles cabs are notoriously unreliable. A swift request for help inevitably brought swift results! I think that was so, because the *Other Side* not only understood my need at the moment, but approved of my purpose, talking on the air about books dealing with spiritual matters.

Years ago, a friend advised me that a pair of unique gold medals of great historical value were going to be auctioned off shortly in New York. The two medals pertained to the personal family history of my former wife Catherine and, of course, our daughters. But my means at the time were very limited, and these two pieces were truly priceless. The competition might drive the price up beyond my means to acquire them and I very much wanted them to stay in the family. I asked for INTER-VENTION, then asked my friend to go to the auction and see what he could do.

When the two medals were called up, my friend noticed a man near him starting to bid. He felt compelled to turn to the man and suggest that someone in the family wanted them, and he would gladly not bid on anything the stranger was keen on. It turned out that my friend was able to purchase the pieces at rock bottom prices. Today, they are overseas, again in the possession of the family of the Counts and Barons Buxhoeveden, where they belong.

Recently, my good friend, the psychic Marisa Anderson, asked me to help a friend of hers, a professional animator who had fallen on hard times despite his skills and track record. Off hand, I had no idea where I could send him, because I have never had any dealings with film animation and don't know the right people in this branch of the industry. I asked for guidance; suddenly, a thought literally jumped into my head about a very successful production company in the animation field in Ireland I had read about in Variety. I remembered the name Sullivan, but the directory did not list such a company over there. I made some calls, and with the help of the Irish Consulate got the new name of the company and all details, which I immediately forwarded to the gentleman who needed the work. Sure enough, it turned out they were very much interested in him.

Clearly, the folks on the *Other Side* understand mundane matters as well as we do; after all, they lived here before!

Recently, a set of circumstances, such as expensive dental work and a number of payments coming together, found me about $3,000 short of cash, despite this having been a pretty good year income-wise. Try as I might, I could not meet the deadlines, because my money would not be in my hands in time. What was I to do, after all avenues I could think of had failed me? Once again, I explained to the *Other Side* what the situation was, what I had tried, and asked for INTERVENTION. A week went by. I looked forward to my deadlines with a sense of embarrassment, if not real concern.

The I received a telephone call, out of left field, so to speak, from a publishing company in New Jersey. It appeared that they had been in possession of a license to publish a separate edition of a book I had written and published in 1967! The license had just run out and they wanted to renew it. They offered me a contract, and a payment of $3,000. I did not even know there was such a license in existence any more, let alone where.

Do not ever invoke intervention for unworthy causes, for evil purposes, or to hurt someone who may have caused you unhappiness. It is never up to you to hand out punishment. The *Other Side* takes care of it if the need arises. The system I am about to explain to you is for positive action: to help you achieve a goal, to protect you from danger, to break through the barrier of ordinary logic because your problem is more important at this moment in earth time.

You achieve a moment of inner peace, if possible, and then you address the *Other Side*:

"Dear Friends (or God, or Lord,) I have a problem. The problem is such and such (describe in a few sentences — not too many — what exactly the problem is). I have tried and failed to solve this problem. Or, this is my need. I have been unable to fulfill this need. INTERVENTION PLEASE!"

That is all. Then change the train of your thoughts immediately. Step back from it and go on with your life. You have made your request for Intervention. Be sure and do NOT speculate about it now, or whether you will get help. Do NOT tell the *Other Side* what it is they should do to help you. If you feel like it, you can end the request for Intervention with this quote John, 11 — "Thank you O Lord for having heard me, I know that thou hearest me always." And that is all.

The call for INTERVENTION may be made for emergencies, for life or death situations, but also for trifles like the immediate need for a taxi. But it must NEVER be general, always be very precise and specific as to what the immediate problem or need is. And do NOT suggest how it should be resolved by the *Other Side*.

It has always worked for me. It will work for you, if you follow these rules precisely and do NOT deviate in any way whatever, do not add anything or change a single word.

You have then found the one direct pipeline to the *Other Side*, directly from you to the Spirit World. Without intermediary. Without need for one. You and The Power, heart to heart.